Many a Midnight Ship

Many a Midnight Ship

TRUE STORIES OF
GREAT LAKES SHIPWRECKS

Mark Bourrie

KEY PORTER BOOKS

Some parts of this work have been adapted from stories previously published in *True Canadian Stories of the Great Lakes* by Mark Bourrie.

Library and Archives Canada Cataloguing in Publication

Bourrie, Mark, 1957–
  Many a midnight ship : true stories of Great Lakes shipwrecks / Mark Bourrie.

ISBN 1-55263-650-X

  1. Shipwrecks—Great Lakes—History. 2. Great Lakes—History. I. Title.

G525.B678 2005   977   C2005-900135-6

The publisher gratefully acknowledges the support of the Canada Council for the Arts and the Ontario Arts Council for its publishing program. We acknowledge the support of the Government of Ontario through the Ontario Media Development Corporation's Ontario Book Initiative.

We acknowledge the financial support of the Government of Canada through the Book Publishing Industry Development Program (BPIDP) for our publishing activities.

Key Porter Books Limited
Six Adelaide Street East, Tenth Floor
Toronto, Ontario
Canada M5C 1H6

www.keyporter.com

Text design: Peter Maher
Electronic formatting: Jean Lightfoot Peters
Printed and bound in Canada

05 06 07 08 09 6 5 4 3 2 1

To Maia, Ian and Megan

Contents

Introduction

*"They know what shipwrecks are, for, out of sight of land,
however inland, they have drowned full many a midnight
ship with all its shrieking crew."*

HERMAN MELVILLE wrote those words about the
Great Lakes in *Moby Dick* in 1851, long before the
wrecks of the *Asia,* the *Eastland,* the *Algoma,* the
Charles Price, the *Lady Elgin,* and the *Edmund Fitzgerald.*
The list of ships sunk in the Great Lakes would fill, by my
rough calculations, fifty pages of a book. Even if one
includes the remnants of the commercial fishing fleets, there
are far more merchant vessels on the bottom of the Great
Lakes than there are floating on their surface.

The same could be said, I suppose, of the English
Channel, the Mediterranean, and the Caribbean, but the
Great Lakes were late arrivals to the marine trade. Ship

traffic really began only after the American Revolution. It was given a huge boost by the opening of the Erie Canal, reached a peak before the Great Depression, and is now in a steep decline. Scheduled passenger runs stopped years ago, except on ferry runs. The railway car ferry trade is long-forgotten. Prairie grain heads overland to Pacific ports, not through the lakes. Boats bearing iron ore still feed the steel mills at Gary, Detroit, the Soo (Sault Ste. Marie), Cleveland, and Hamilton, but those mills are being strangled by foreign competition. Harbors are being built up with waterfront skyscrapers, grain elevators are coming down, and evolution goes on.

In the movie *Field of Dreams*, Thomas Mann, the bitter writer played by James Earl Jones, has a revelation: "America has rolled by like an army of steamrollers. It's been erased like a blackboard, rebuilt, and erased again." Baseball, he says, "has been the one constant, reminding us of all that once was good, and that could be again." There have been other constants, of course, and, as a Canadian, I've got to argue that hockey's near the top of that list. But the real constant in North America is the desire to defeat distance, to develop technologies to communicate instantly, to do business without the inconvenience of space, to travel quickly. Military historian John Keegan says Europeans battle against time, North Americans struggle with distance. We adapted our technology to use the Great Lakes as a highway and then, without much evident regret, we've left the boats behind and taken to airplanes and cars. Our belongings are shipped by truck or by plane. People today would not even think of traveling by boat between Chicago and Buffalo. They just don't have time.

So, in most ways, the age of the Great Lakes ship is over. Certainly, the age of the ship disaster has passed. As of this writing, it's been thirty years since the *Edmund Fitzgerald* sank. That was the last and most famous Great Lakes shipwreck. When the Fitz was lost, nine years had passed since the previous big wreck, the *James Morrell*, went down in Lake Huron. But, in the decades before, three or four lake freighters were lost every year, often with their entire crew. Somehow, life has become more valuable. Modern ships are better built and more money is spent on technology that saves lives. With luck the record will hold, and the Fitz will be the last big one lost.

I've learned a few things since I wrote *Ninety Fathoms Down* in 1995, updating and adding to it for *True Canadian Stories of the Great Lakes* in 2004, and writing this book. For instance, when I see a disaster movie like *Titanic* that shows relieved sailors and passengers getting into lifeboats in the open seas, I think of the *Asia*, the *Sand Merchant*, the *Morrell*, the *Carl Bradley*, the *Marquette and Bessemer No. 2*, and many other Great Lakes ships whose survivors, trapped in lifeboats in the open lakes, came to envy those who had stayed on board the lost ships.

It must baffle people who've never lived near the Great Lakes that full-size ships can sink without a trace in lakes that are 500 feet above sea level and more than a thousand miles from the ocean. The idea that you can drive for more than a day from the East Coast through farmland, mountains and cities, then come to bodies of water that are so large that they stretch far, far off over the horizon, must be hard for newcomers to understand. Certainly the marine explorer Jacques Cousteau and his sons had that feeling when they almost lost their ship, *Calypso*, on Georgian Bay on the way back from filming the wreck of the *Edmund Fitzgerald*. Cousteau thought the expedition would be a yachting trip. He arrived at Quebec City saying he never wanted to challenge the lakes again.

Now the lakes are left to pleasure boats, a few lake and ocean freighters, cottagers, campers, fishermen, families who worship beaches. Some of us are wistful when we think of the past. Some of us long for the days when it was possible to see the five big lakes by water. Still, we're here because of those who went before us, and we live in conditions of comfort, safety, and luxury that were utterly unknown a century ago. Some of us look back with envy, but those people who opened up the Great Lakes country would have been quick to trade places with us. Our challenge is to ensure that, one hundred years from now, people look back on us with nostalgia, not envy.

CHAPTER ONE

Brawling on Lake Erie

ROBERT BARCLAY was born on September 18, 1786 into a mainly peaceful world. The monarchies of Europe had achieved a delicate balance of power. A czar ruled Russia, a king reigned in France, and England, whose monarch, George III, suffered from bouts of madness, was run by a parliament dominated by solid conservatives. On the other side of the Atlantic, the United States had gained its independence and was turned inward while its leaders wrote a constitution.

Three years later, the peaceful equilibrium was disturbed by a rebellion of the French bourgoisie that clipped the wings of the country's king. When Barclay was six, the revolution fell into the hands of extremists who sent the king to the guillotine. By the time Robert was ten, Napoleon was redrawing the borders of Europe.

Robert was raised in a middle-class family in Fife,

Scotland. His father was an Anglican priest. His mother's brother, however, was Admiral William Duddingston, a famous hero. This familial touch of naval glory must have rubbed off on the growing boy. As Napoleon's armies conquered much of Europe, the Royal Navy sent its press gangs through the port towns looking for men and boys for involuntary careers on His Majesty's ships. Barclay, because of his class, was in a position to avoid this form of slavery but, at the age of twelve, he announced to his parents that he wanted to join the navy.

The Barclays disapproved of his choice. In spite of his forbear's illustrious naval career, they believed their son would be better advised to make a career for himself in the Church, the universities, or the civil service. His grades were good, he was handsome and personable, and the family had important connections. The Navy was generally the refuge for second sons and misfits, not young gentlemen. But, in those days, they could legally do nothing to interfere with their twelve-year-old's decision.

In the summer of 1798, Barclay was appointed a midshipman on board a forty-four-gun frigate, HMS *Anson*. The Napoleonic conflict had developed into a world war, and the *Anson* was on the hunt for French ships. On that first cruise, the *Anson* captured two French frigates, two large Spanish gunboats, a privateer, and seven merchant vessels. This made the voyage profitable as well as exciting. While enemy ships sent to the bottom enhanced a crew's pride and reputation, captured ships were worth hard cash: the British government paid bonuses for prizes towed into British ports.

Six years into his career, Robert Barclay sat for his officer exams and, in March, 1805, he was raised to lieutenant (his commission signed by Horatio Nelson). He was appointed to the *Swiftsure*, a full-sized ship of the line.

The promotion was perfectly timed. On October 21, 1805 Lord Nelson, with twenty-seven line of battle ships, crushed a superior French and Spanish fleet off Cape Trafalgar, Spain, destroying seventeen enemy ships and capturing the rest of the fleet. The *Swiftsure* went one-on-one with the *Achilles*, one of the most powerful French ships, and had just seventeen killed or wounded before the *Achilles* struck her flag. The *Swiftsure* won even more glory by rescuing prize crews that had been given command of captured French ships when a hurricane struck the fleet just days after the battle.

After Trafalgar, Barclay returned to Fife where he successfully wooed Agnes Cossar. It was to be a long, long-distance engagement. Just before Christmas, 1807, Barclay was posted to the frigate *Diana*, which hunted merchantmen trying to run the English blockade of French ports. While the *Diana* was smaller than the *Swiftsure*, she stood a very good chance of capturing prizes. The next April, the *Diana* caught a French convoy trying to sneak along the coast to Rochefort. The enemy ships ducked into the little port of Noirmoutier. Barclay was tapped to head a commando raid to go after them. The French were vigilant, however, and as Barclay and his men tried to creep up to the French merchantman where it was anchored, a ball from a well-aimed swivel cannon took off the young man's left arm.

The injury didn't end Barclay's naval career but, for the next four years, he was kept out of the center of the action. In 1809, he was stationed in the backwater of Halifax, Nova Scotia. Three years later, war broke out between Britain and the United States. Barclay, against his own best judgment, was shipped to Lake Erie, where the situation for the British was very grim.

The War of 1812 was primarily a series of naval skirmishes rather than a struggle between armies. A glance at a map shows why. There is no place between Cornwall, on the St. Lawrence River, and the Pigeon River, west of Lake Superior, where the border can be crossed on foot, except in winter. The waterways were both a barrier and a highway. The navy that controlled the lakes could transport soldiers and supplies to their enemy's shore. They could choose the time and place of battle and tie up large numbers of the enemy's troops. Napoleon, fighting his own wars at this time, said England's control of the English Channel tied up 300,000 of his soldiers in worthless forts and defensive positions along France's coast. In the same way, in North America, the country that controlled the lakes could maintain the web of communications between isolated forts at the strategic places where the Great Lakes join each other and choke off the enemy's movements and supplies in what the Americans called "The Old Northwest." No country could score a decisive victory when its opponent controlled the lakes.

At the beginning of the war, both sides had only a few merchant schooners on the lakes. Consequently, during the two years of struggle, they raced to build fleets that would give them the upper hand. Every conceivable vessel was pressed into service. Obsolete cannon, elderly fur trappers—anyone and anything that could add strength to the fleets were requisitioned. Then they started building real warships but, for Barclay, it was almost impossible to pry the sailors and supplies he needed from the over-stretched Royal Navy.

The only British navy yard on the upper lakes was at Amherstburg, on the Detroit River. Here, Barclay oversaw construction of the last and biggest ship to be built in the yard, the HMS *Detroit*, named for General Isaac Brock's bloodless capture of Fort Detroit in 1812. Construction began in January, 1813, but progress was fitful, since Barclay lacked the skilled carpenters and essential supplies to do the job. These deficiencies were made worse when sails, ropes, and much other equipment en route to Amherstburg were destroyed by the Americans who captured and burned York on April 27, 1813. And, even when the *Detroit* was finished, Barclay had a tough time finding a crew to sail her. The young officer was forced to teach basic sailing skills to the soldiers who guarded the yard and to some of the local traders.

The completion of the ship in early September gave the British five vessels in addition to the *Detroit* (which became Barclay's flagship): the ship *Queen Charlotte*, the brig *Hunter*, the schooners *Lady Prevost* and *Chippawa*, and the sloop *Little Belt*. Another vessel, the *Nancy*, which tried to join them from Lake Huron, was driven off by American cannon set up at the entrance to the St. Clair River.

Barclay's opposite number had fewer practical problems but still was plagued by worry and prone to be suspicious. Oliver Hazard Perry was born on August 23, 1785, at South Kingstown, near the village of Wakefield, Rhode Island. Like Barclay, he was well-connected: his father and uncle both were United States Navy captains. Perry was enlisted as a thirteen-year-old midshipman in the U.S. Navy on April 7, 1799. He saw action against the French in the near-war of 1799, and then sailed to the Mediterranean to fight the Barbary Pirates along the shores of Tripoli. In April, 1809, he was seen as a comer and given his first command, the fourteen-gun schooner *Revenge*.

His luck changed, however, in January, 1811 when the *Revenge* struck a reef near Watch Hill Point and went down. Perry was exonerated by the subsequent court martial (which is held in most navies after a ship is sunk or surrendered), but the loss of the ship—and the fact the United States was still at peace—hobbled Perry's career. He was out of work until the spring of 1812. He used the interlude to marry and start a family.

During the first months of the war, Perry worked on a small ship patrolling the New England coast but, by the end of 1812, he had pulled enough strings to get a front-line posting to Lake Erie. Perry believed aggressive action on the Great Lakes would salvage his career. He and the lead shipwright Noah Brown of New York, who had learned his trade from the British, drove his men hard to build six ships at the navy yard in Erie, Pennsylvania. By the next summer, the tradesmen sent to Erie from Philadelphia had built a tough little fleet. Cannon and anchors to outfit them were dragged through the bush by oxcart. Sailors made the long walk inland from Pittsburgh and helped crew the fleet. This fleet consisted of four fast, armed schooners, and the two brigs, *Lawrence* and *Niagara*. In late spring, Perry added five converted merchant ships.

On August 1, Perry aboard the *Lawrence* took his fleet out of Erie and prepared to meet the British. He set up a base at Put-In Bay, near Sandusky, Ohio, and watched the mouth of the Detroit River for Barclay's squadron.

On September 9, Barclay' fleet cast off from the Amherstburg wharf and drifted down the Detroit River. The next morning, the fleets were within sight of each other. The ships' masters spent two hours tacking for the best position before finally beginning their exchange of fire just before noon. The *Detroit* drew first blood, nailing the *Lawrence* just ahead of midship. The *Chippawa* joined in to help rake the *Lawrence* with grapeshot and cannonballs. The *Queen Charlotte*, meanwhile, was being punished by the *Niagara* and *Caledonia*, killing her commander and first officer. The Battle of Lake Erie was turning into a very bloody fight.

Perry flew a flag upon which were written Captain James Lawrence's dying words, "Don't give up the ship." Earlier that year, Lawrence's men aboard the *Chesapeake* had ignored that command and surrendered to the British man-of-war *Leopard*. Now the *Lawrence* was about to do likewise. At 2:30, Perry abandoned the crippled *Lawrence*, and dodged British bullets as his longboat made for the *Niagara*. That ship, which hadn't been able to maneuver to an advantageous position, was out of the battle at the start and was untouched when Perry boarded here. He moved the *Niagara* within range of the *Detroit* and opened fire. A canister shot struck Barclay's shoulder blade, ripping apart his one good arm. Some of his sailors stumbled over their dead crewmates as they carried their wounded captain below. The second-in-command, Lieutenant Inglis, took charge.

The *Detroit*'s port guns had been blasted from their carriages and most of their gunners were dead. Inglis tried to turn the *Detroit* to bring his starboard guns to bear on the *Niagara*. The British frigate *Queen Charlotte* was trying to make the same maneuver. The rigging of the two ships became tangled, and they both were now at the mercy of the *Niagara*. The *Lady Prevost*, the only ship that might have saved them, was already battered. Her captain, standing on the deck with a gaping wound in his back, tried to make the turn, but, before he could do so, the two larger British ships had struck their colors, effectively ending the battle. Just fifteen minutes had elapsed since Perry climbed on board the *Niagara*. He returned to the *Lawrence* to receive the British surrender from the few remaining uninjured officers, gallantly refusing the swords that they offered, and then penned his famous message to General William Harrison:

We have met the enemy and they are ours:
Two Ships, two Brigs, one Schooner & one Sloop.
Yours, with great respect and esteem
O.H. Perry

After the battle all ships dropped anchor. Sailors began repairing the shredded riggings and clearing the shattered timbers from the decks. In the first hours after the battle, most of the wounded received very little help. The Battle of Lake Erie was exceptionally bloody, made worse by the fact that almost all the wounds were caused by close-quarter cannon fire. Most of the wounded suffered injuries that could be treated only by amputation or major surgery. The dead sailors were buried at sea that night, while the officers from both sides were interred together on South Bass Island the next day.

Dr. Usher Parsons was one of the very few physicians in Perry's fleet. He found himself in the midst of a medical disaster. Parsons' account of the battle and its aftermath was published in the *New England Journal of Medicine* in October, 1818:

About 12 o'clock, on a clear pleasant day, we met the enemy. The action soon became general and was severely felt; especially on board the Lawrence, the flag ship; two of the enemy's largest vessels engaging her, at a short distance, for nearly two hours; part of which time the men fell on board of her faster than they could be taken below. The vessel being shallow built afforded no cockpit or place of shelter for the wounded; they were therefore received on the ward room floor, which was about on a level with the surface of the water.

Being only nine or ten feet square, this floor was soon covered, which made it necessary to pass the wounded out into another apartment, as fast as the bleeding could be stanched either by Ligatures or tourniquet. Indeed this was all that was attempted for their benefit during the engagement, except that in some instances division was made of a small portion of flesh, by which a dangling limb that annoyed the patient, was hanging from the body. Several, after receiving this treatment, were again wounded, among whom was midshipman Lamb, who was moving from me with a tourniquet on the arm when he received a cannon ball in the chest; and a seaman brought down with both arms fractured, was afterwards struck by a cannon ball in the chest and in both lower extremities.

An hour's engagement had so far swept the deck, that new appeals for surgical aid were less frequent; a remission at this time, very desirable both to the wounded and myself; for the repeated request of the Commodore, to spare him another man had taken from me the last one I had to assist in moving the wounded. In fact many of the wounded themselves took the deck again at this critical moment. Our prospects nevertheless darkened, every new visitor from the deck bringing tidings still more dismal than the last, till finally it was announced that we had struck. The effect of this on the wounded was distressing in the extreme; medical aid was rejected and little else could be heard from them than "sink the ship"—"let us all sink together." But this state of despair was short. The Commodore, who was still unhurt, had gone on board the Niagara and, with the small vessels bearing down upon the enemy, soon brought down the flags of their two heaviest ships, and thus changed the horrors of defeat into shouts of victory. But all the wounded were not permitted to mingle in the joy. The gallant Brooks, and some others were no more. They were too much exhausted by their wounds, to survive the confusions that immediately preceded this happy transition.

The action terminated shortly after three o'clock and, of about one hundred men reported fit for duty in the morning, twenty-one were found dead, and sixty-three wounded. The wounded arteries occupied my first attention, all which, except where amputation was required, were rendered secure before dark. Having no assistant (the surgeon on board with me being very sick) I deemed it safer to defer amputating till morning, and in the mean time suffered the tourniquets to remain on the limbs. Nothing more was done through the night than to administer opiates and preserve shattered limbs in a uniform position. At daylight a subject was on the table for amputation of the thigh, and at eleven o'clock all amputations were finished. The impatience of this class of the wounded, to meet the operation, rendered it necessary to take them in the same succession in which they fell. The compound and simple fractures were next attended to, then luxations, lacerations, and contusions, all which occupied my time till twelve o'clock at night.

The day following I visited the wounded of the *Niagara*, who had lain till that time with their wounds undressed. I found the surgeon sick in bed with hands too feeble to execute the dictates of a feeling heart. Twenty-one wounded were mustered, most of whom were taken on board the *Lawrence* and dressed, and afterwards such as were lying in like manner on board the small vessels. In the course of the evening the sick were prescribed for, which was the first attention I had been able to render them since the action.

The whole number of wounded in the squadron was ninety-six. Of these, twenty-five were cases of compound fracture: viz: of the arm, six; of the thigh, four; of the leg, eight; of the shoulder, three; of the ribs, three; and skull, one. Of simple fracture, there were four cases: viz. of the thigh, leg, arm and ribs. Grapeshot wounds, large and small were thirty-seven. There were two cases of concussion of the brain; three of the chest, and two of the pelvis. The contusions, large and small, were ten, and sprains, six.

Of the whole number, three died; viz: midshipman Claxton with compound fractures of the shoulder, in which a part of the clavicle, scapula, and humerus was carried away; a seaman with a mortification of the lower extremity, in which there had been a compound fracture, and another with a fracture of the skull, where a part of the cerebral substance was destroyed.

The compound fractures of the extremities were much retarded in their cure, by the frequent displacement of the bones, by the motion of the ship in rough weather, or by some other unlucky disturbance of the limb. In this way the bones in one case did not unite, until after forty days had elapsed, and in two or three other cases, not till after twenty-five days. The delay of amputations already mentioned had no effect on the success of the operations. Every case did well.

There were not more than two very singular wounds, or such as would be unlikely to occur in any sea engagement. In one of these cases a grapeshot four times as large as a musket ball, passed under the pyramidal muscle, without injuring the peritoneum. In the other, a canister shot twice the size of a musket ball entered the eye, and on the fifth or sixth day was detected at the inside angle of the lower jaw and cut out. In its passage it must have fractured the orbitar sphenoid bone, and passing under the temporal arch, inside the coronal process of the lower jaw, must have done great injury to the temporal muscle, and other soft parts, lying in its way.

The recovery of so great a proportion of the wounded

may in a great measure be attributed to the following causes: First to the purity of the air. The patients were ranged along the upper deck, with no other shelter from the weather than a high awning to shade them. They continued in this situation for a fortnight, and when taken on shore, were placed in very spacious apartments, well ventilated. Secondly, to the supply of food best adapted to their cases, as fowls, fresh meat, milk, eggs and vegetables in abundance. The second day after the action, the farmers on the Ohio shore brought along side every article of the above description that could be desired. Thirdly, to the happy state of mind which victory occasioned. The observations which I have been able to make on the wounded of three engagements have convinced me that this state of mind has greater effect than has generally been supposed; and that the surgeon on the conquering side will always be more successful, than the one who has charge of the vanquished crew. Lastly, to the assistance rendered me by Commodore Perry and Mr. Davidson. The latter gentleman was a volunteer soldier among the Kentucky troops and engaged to serve on board the fleet during the action. After the action he rendered the wounded every aid in his power, continuing with them three months. And the commodore seemed quite as solicitous for their welfare as he could possibly felt for the success of the battle.

Although Barclay was well enough to meet Perry after the battle, because of the new wound in his right arm, he would be severely incapacitated for life. Barclay was patched up by a ship's surgeon, but nothing could be done to salvage the muscles in his shoulder. Two days after the defeat, he called an officer into his cabin and dictated an account for the British admiralty. It ended "I trust that although unsuccessful, you will approve of the motives that induced me to sail, under so many disadvantages and that it may be hereafter proved, that under such circumstances the Honor of His Majesty's Flag has not been tarnished."

After the crew was taken off and interned, the *Detroit* spent the winter of 1813–14 in Put-in-Bay. She was then brought to Presque Isle. Like almost all of the naval vessels of the War of 1812, the *Detroit*, along with the *Queen Charlotte* and the *Lawrence*, were "laid up in waiting" with their masts removed. As the years passed without another war the ships were allowed to fill with water and sink.

The court martial of Robert Barclay took place September 9, 1814 on board His Majesty's Ship *Gladiator* in the harbor at Portsmouth, England. Admiral Edward James Foote presided. Barclay was present, along with his officers. They had been paroled by the Americans—released after promising to remain non-combatants in the war— soon after the battle. The court decision, favorable to Barclay, said:

> That the Capture of His Majesty's late Squadron was
> caused by the very defective Means Captain Barclay pos-
> sessed to equip them on Lake Erie the Want of a
> sufficient Number of able Seamen whom he had repeat-
> edly and earnestly requested to be sent to him the very
> great Superiority of the force of the Enemy to the British
> Squadron and the unfortunate early fall of the superior
> Officers in the Action. That it appears that the greatest

Exertions had been made by Captain Barclay in equip-
ping and getting into Order the Vessels under his
Command That he was fully justified under the existing
circumstances in bringing the Enemy to Action. That the
Judgment and Gallantry of Captain Barclay in taking his
Squadron into Action and during the Contest were
highly conspicuous and entitled him to the highest Praise
and that the whole of the Officers and Men of His
Majesty's late Squadron conducted themselves in the
most gallant Manner and doth adjudge the said Captain
Robert Heriot Barclay his surviving Officers and Men to
be most fully and most honorably acquitted and they are
hereby most fully and most honorably acquitted
accordingly.

Barclay, despite his exoneration, had to wait seven years for
promotion to captain, and even then, it gained him little.
He spent only a few months at sea after his repatriation.
Because of his injuries, he offered his fiancé the chance to
back out of her engagement but he and Agnes went ahead
with the marriage. The couple lived at Saxe-Coburg House
in Edinburgh where Barclay died in 1837.

Despite the glory heaped on him for being the first
American commander to win a major naval action and the
only officer, up until that time, to compel the surrender of a
British squadron, Perry fared little better than his British
opponents and, in fact, predeceased them. By the end of the
war, it had become obvious to U.S. authorities that Perry

was a problem. In 1815, he was sent to the Mediterranean for another bout with the Barbary pirates. While his ship, the man-of-war *Java*, was taking on supplies in Italy, Perry argued with his Marines commander, John Heath, and slapped the officer in the face. Both officers were court-martialed and found guilty, but got off with a reprimand. However, even in 1815, it was injudicious to humiliate a Marine. Heath challenged Perry to a duel, which was subsequently fought on October 19, 1817, on the same field where Aaron Burr killed Alexander Hamilton. The Marine fired first from four paces and missed. Honor was satisfied when Perry refused to pull the trigger.

Perry became embroiled in Navy politics. To get rid of him, President James Monroe sent the headstrong young officer on a diplomatic mission to South America. On August 17, 1819, he died of a fever that decimated his men as they sailed on the Orinoco River.

Nor did the ships fare well, at least in the short term. The *Detroit*'s cannon were salvaged as souvenirs. One is kept at Erie's Maritime Museum and her flags are trophies of war at the U.S. Naval Academy in Annapolis, Maryland. The *Niagara* served as station ship in Erie until 1820, and then joined the *Detroit* at the bottom of Misery Bay.

The ghost of the *Niagara* lived on, however, and was given a new home in a reconstructed version. Timbers from the original *Niagara* were salvaged and built into the walls of the replica, which is operated by the Pennsylvania Historical Society as a sail-training vessel.

There's now also a replica of the *Detroit* working out of Fort Malden, the Canadian historic site at Amherstburg. The ship's real fate was truly grim. The same year Barclay died, the *Detroit* was raised from the bottom of Misery Bay and sold. For three years, she worked as a merchant ship, but in 1841 the leaking hulk was bought by a group of merchants in Niagara Falls, New York. Repeating a stunt that was always a hit with tourists, the new owners loaded the ship with animals and sent her down the rapids toward the falls as a popular, if grotesque, and profoundly inhumane spectacle.

Maybe it was the ship's own pride or the ghost of Barclay at the helm, but the *Detroit* drifted toward rocks and was hung up in the rapids until the current tore her apart denying the spectators the thrilling crash they had anticipated and paid for. Legend has it that not a scrap of the *Detroit* was ever found.

CHAPTER TWO

The Witch of November

ONLY THE VERY SUPERSTITIOUS believe in curses, Jonahs, jinxes, ghost vessels—and the Witch of November. And even the superstitious know in their hearts that the blackest of clouds is without malice, the most savage wind is a random force of nature, and that a storm is just a storm. Some storms, of course, are worse than others. And because November storms are often the worst of all, they have acquired an evil reputation.

More ships have been lost on the Great Lakes in November than in any other month. The last-minute run before freeze-up, the sunny day that masks the coming of a gale-force blizzard, both are known end-of-season hazards. The short days and long dark nights of November have affected the judgment, sapped the courage, and snapped short the lives of too many sailors. And there's always another ship's master who thinks he can outrun a building storm.

In spite of what we know when we look at the facts rationally, it's easy to see how the legend of the November Witch has taken hold and been perpetuated. Singer and songwriter Gordon Lightfoot was tapping into a rich myth when he wrote his evocative ballad, "The Wreck of the *Edmund Fitzgerald.*"

The Witch took her first known victim in 1781, when the British navy ship *Ontario* went to the bottom of the lake she was named for. The loss of the *Ontario* is still mysterious. There's no firm figure on the loss of life. The wreck has never been found (though some hints have surfaced lately). No one is sure of the real nature of her last trip.

Officially, she was taking Colonel Bolton, commander of Fort Niagara, home. Bolton shipped out on the *Ontario* on the morning of October 31. The post's military band marched ahead and, as this little parade reached the dock, the rest of the passengers fell in: thirty five members of the 35th Infantry regiment; four women and five children, members of the families of 38th infantrymen; two members of the 8th regiment; two Loyalists from Butler's Rangers, a notorious Tory regiment hated by the people of New York state; four Natives; a ship's gunner; and two officers of the King's artillery. The ship they boarded was commanded by Captain James Andrews, assisted by his first mate, Lieutenant Plau, and had a crew of twenty-nine.

At least that's the number in the official reports: eighty-seven people in total. But were there more? It seems likely that there were, and the real number may have been kept secret for a tactical, military reason. A week before the *Ontario* left port, British soldiers had foiled an American raid on British boats at Oswego. Tipped off that Captain Joshua Voorman and sixty of his men were on their way, the British had sprung a trap, killing four of the Americans, and taking the rest prisoner, including Voorman. Some twenty of the Americans, men who couldn't tell which way the political wind was blowing, joined the British, leaving thirty-six unaccounted for.

During the American Revolution, neither side was particularly kind to captured enlisted men, but officers, such as Voorman, were given comfortable billets and held for exchange. Voorman, however, disappears from the historical record, as do most of the men under his command. Was he on the *Ontario*? It was common practice for prisoners to be moved from important posts like Fort Niagara to less accessible backwaters. And it was usual to send word to the enemy that a captured officer was being moved. But the British would not have wanted to reveal that the *Ontario* had been lost. Not only was its sinking an embarrassment, but it was also a strategic blow that further weakened the British at a time when their chances of winning the war were already dim, at best.

Even when Voorman and his men are added to the total of eighty-seven known to have been on board, this brings the new total to just 113, far fewer than the 300 said by many writers to have been lost with the ship. Perhaps the secrecy surrounding the voyage itself is to blame for the confusion. People are more likely to inflate numbers when there are rumors in circulation.

The British knew, of course, that the sinking of the *Ontario* could not be covered up indefinitely—especially in a time when the loss of any ship, least of all a warship, was important news. At most, they could hope only to buy some time until the lake froze and a new warship could be built to take its place. But by spreading disinformation, they sowed the seed of historical error. The *Ontario*, as large as she was, has become a much bigger ship over time. Rumors that she carried a load of treasure were being spread within months of her sinking. Casualty figures of 300 found their way into the history books and the true story of the loss of *Ontario*, dramatic as it was, entered the realm of ghost ship tales.

The *Ontario*'s fate was sealed in the doldrums off the coast of Africa when a vertical column of hot, moist air rose above the calm sea in the late summer of 1781. Cool air was drawn in to replace it. Energy from the rotation of the Earth caused this tropical depression to begin moving clockwise, gathering more moist air and energy into it as the storm caught the westerly trades and headed for the Lesser Antilles. This tropical depression developed into a massive storm, probably a Category 5 hurricane, before it made landfall. Ships' captains watched the mercury in their barometers plummet and raced for shelter. This storm, however, had the power to shatter ships in harbors as well as on the high seas. It clawed its way along the southeastern edge of the Caribbean, sinking four British warships at St. Lucia, and swamping another British ship of fifty guns at St. Vincent.

Losing none of its fury, the storm took forty French ships at Martinique. At least 300 men were killed on just one new man-of-war. Then the storm moved northward, through waters crowded with the ships of wartime Britain's Caribbean squadron and the busy West Indies trade. A dozen more warships, and at least 100 British merchant ships were lost. These astonishing figures are drawn from British Admiralty records and the claims made to Lloyd's of London, whose re-insurers were nearly broken by the losses. No one knows how many uninsured French, Spanish, Dutch, and American ships were lost, or how many people died in the towns along the coasts of Puerto Rico, Haiti, Cuba, and the Bahamas. It was the worst hurricane ever recorded, and it likely changed the balance of naval power in the western hemisphere.

Next, following the Gulf Stream, the storm veered northeast, mauling sea traffic along the main sea route to Europe. For four days, it disappears from the historical record, since no one who was in the storm as it moved 300 miles off the coast of the United States lived to describe it. Unlike most other hurricanes, which lose force as they head north, this one appears to have grown even stronger, perhaps because it was hemmed in by cool high-pressure systems. Its later movements suggest there was a high that blocked the storm from continuing along the Gulf Stream toward Newfoundland. At Bermuda, it consumed eighteen ships before heading north to New England and over Montreal, expending much of its energy in the woods of Quebec and Labrador before catching the jet stream to bring rain showers to Britain, where admirals and shipping company owners still had no idea of its existence as a hurricane or of the horrific losses of life, ships, and money that it had brought about.

There was no system to warn of approaching hurricanes in the late eighteenth century. Sailors knew that fall was hurricane season. By tracing wind patterns and watching their barometers, they could tell if stormy weather was moving in. But hurricanes moved much faster than news in those days.

When this storm hit Lake Ontario, no one had any inkling that it was coming. Fall storms, especially just after the September equinox and at the outbreak of winter weather in mid-November, are predictable, but hurricanes rarely make it to the Great Lakes. By the time they do cross the low mountain ranges between the Atlantic and Great Lakes basins, they are almost always weakened to tropical storms or tropical depressions. A true hurricane on the Great Lakes is, perhaps, a twice-a-century occurrence.

It was bad luck that the *Ontario* sailed into the path of this freak storm. A good captain could bring his ship through a tropical storm, but only a very lucky one could out-sail a hurricane, and this storm was one of the most powerful hurricanes of the century. Captain Andrews was not that lucky. And he was handicapped by the design of the ship he commanded. At best, he had a warship designed for the high seas, a ship that was not engineered for the different wave configurations of the lakes. It may have been too flat in the keel. It was certainly heavy with cargo and people. Even if the lowest estimate of about ninety passengers and crew is accurate, the ship was loaded with the baggage of the families of the soldiers, Colonel Bolton's belongings, and whatever the natives brought with them, along with other soldiers' kit, cannon, and ammunition. If there were more men aboard, the prisoners of Voorman's unit for instance, the estimate of total tonnage must be increased. As well, any cargo loaded for the garrison of Carleton Island, the *Ontario*'s destination, added to the *Ontario*'s weight and subsequent troubles. And Captain Andrews was in a hurry. He wanted to make Fort Oswego (still in British hands) in the early hours of October 31, pick up members of a Butler's

Rangers raiding party, and sail across the lake to Carleton Island, to arrive on the afternoon of the same day.

The wind was with him when he left Fort Niagara. The *Ontario*, under full sail, was making six knots when she was last seen in the afternoon of October 31. When the hurricane struck, the wind switched sharply from the southwest to the northeast. British regular and irregular troops camped on shore spoke of a wall of wind and water that suddenly swept down on them, uprooted trees, carried away their shelters, even blew away their firewood. The roar was so intense the men could not hear each other's shouts. The storm pounded the shore with waves and foam all through the night. Almost certainly, somewhere in the middle of Lake Ontario in the late afternoon or early evening, the *Ontario* was knocked over by the squall line at the edge of the storm. Her rigging would have been torn to pieces, her masts snapped in half, ropes and sail turned into an uncontrollable tangle.

It is likely that the wall of wind and water struck before the crew had time to knock down the ship's sails. Despite the many drills practiced by sailors in the eighteenth and nineteenth centuries, it took skill, luck, and courage to pull down the sails of a large sailing ship in the face of a fast-moving squall. Once the boat began capsizing, her decks would be crammed with fallen and displaced canvas, rope, and broken masts. Water would rush in through her gunports, loading her hull with even more weight to drag her down. As the *Ontario* reared over, water flowed into her net-covered hatches, filling the hold within seconds. The empty lifeboats (perhaps towed by the *Ontario*, rather than stowed on her crowded decks), Captain Andrew's hat, and the few bodies that were found in the days after the storm suggest that passengers were taken by surprise and that the ship sank quickly. The wreck has never been found.

Nothing beats the Great Storm of 1913 for the sheer number of ships and sailors lost. The storm, a freak combination of two powerful weather systems, brought to the Great Lakes just about every kind of unpleasant and dangerous atmospheric element: blinding hail, sleet, snow, and hurricane-force winds. Some of the lowest barometric levels in the history of Great Lakes region meteorology were recorded in the middle of the storm, but most barometers in the worst of it ended up on the bottoms of lakes Huron, Michigan, and Superior. Survivors who witnessed the storm's fury on the open lakes talked of gigantic waves, some as high as sixty feet. These accounts sound exaggerated, but they are so widespread and numerous that it is hard to believe that they're fabricated.

The storm lasted for four days—with sustained hurricane intensity for sixteen hours, much longer than a Caribbean cyclone. The storm piled water into gigantic waves that drove freighters hundreds of yards inshore or took ships to the bottom of the lakes, almost always with all hands. The waves rolled along lake freighters' decks, laying down coats of ice on wheelhouses, rigging, and railings, or they drove against the ships' sides, rolling them over. The storm was laced with snow that lay, after the storm, eight feet deep on the streets of Windsor, Detroit, London, and Cleveland.

"We never had a letup from the time we left Duluth," Captain Story of the Canadian Pacific passenger ship *Assiniboia* told a reporter from a Fort William newspaper. The reporter sent his article across what was left of the telegraph system before the storm moved south and stripped the wires from the poles. "The gale blew fifty miles an hour all the way down Superior," the captain said. "The ice gathered fast on our boat. It was necessary at times to thaw it away in the front of our wheelhouse in order to see. The furious wind, coupled with the freezing temperature, made it one of the fiercest trips I have ever seen."

On Lake Superior, the *Leafield* and the *Henry B. Smith* disappeared with their crews. Three men died on the stranded *William Notting*, lost on Parisian Island. The largest of the Great Lakes claimed the lives of forty-four men during the Great Storm.

A few sailors were lucky enough to survive, but they still took a mauling from the storm. For example, wind and waves battered the cabin, masts, and smokestack of the American carrier *L.C. Waldo* for hours. Captain J. W. Duddleson managed to bring the badly damaged ship close to shore, navigating with a pocket compass illuminated by an oil lamp. He tried to steer between Gull Rock and Manitou Island by listening to the sound of the waves crashing on the rocks, but after eighteen hours his skill and luck ran out. The ship hit the rocks and began to break up. The twenty-six men and two women aboard the *Waldo* huddled on the deck of the fore section for ninety hours waiting for help. At night, they had no lights. There was no radio on board and the ship's flares were lost. As the waves washed over the decks, the crew tied themselves to the *Waldo*'s railings and hatch covers.

Finally, the steamer *Stephenson* went to her aid, but couldn't get close enough to take the crew off. For seven hours, the *Stephenson* maneuvered around the wreck, trying to position herself so that boats could be lowered to rescue the *Waldo*'s crew. The rocks nearly caught the *Stephenson* several times until, finally, her captain gave up. She backed away and called for help from the Portage lifesaving unit on the upper peninsula of Michigan. With the help of a tug, the volunteer Portage lifesavers rescued all of *Waldo*'s crew.

Ten sailors were lost in Lake Michigan, most of them on the barge *Plymouth*, which was cut loose at the height of the storm by the boat that was supposed to be towing her. A U.S. marshal aboard the *Plymouth* damned those who had left him to die. The terrified, angry man took a laundry bill and asked a more composed crew member to write a note to his wife on the back of it. It read:

Dear Wife and Children,
We were left up here Lake Michigan by McKinnon, captain [of the] *J.H. Martin*, tug anchor. He went away and never said goodbye or anything to us. One man lost yesterday. We have been in storm forty hours. Goodbye little ones. I might see you in Heaven. Pray for me.
    Chris K.
    PS. I felt so bad I had another man write for me. Goodbye forever.

The note was washed ashore in a bottle eleven days after the storm.

On Lake Huron, the winds seemed to have a murderous intelligence. After two days of blowing from the northwest, they shifted to the northeast. Ships that had taken refuge in the lee of the American shore suddenly found themselves hammered by hurricane-force gusts that pushed them toward land. Survivors said the waves looked like great black walls that rolled out of the blizzard and washed completely over their ships.

The *Wexford*, a 257-foot package freight carrier built at Sunderland, England in 1883, left Fort William with a crew of eighteen. The Wexford nearly made her destination of Goderich, Ontario with 96,000 bushels of wheat. No one saw the ship after she left the Soo, but the first clue to her fate came just after the storm, when five dead Wexford crewmen washed ashore near the village of St. Joseph, Ontario. People along the Lake Huron shore could hear the *Wexford*'s frantic whistle call but no one could save its crew.

In the past few years, divers have been able to solve many of the mysteries of the Great Storm. In 2000, Grand Bend-based diver Don Chalmers, a retired autoworker, used a fish-finder to locate the Wexford off Point Franks in seventy-five feet of water. She sits upright, her hull covered in zebra mussels but otherwise well preserved. A crew headed by Bob Carey used Goderich as home port for unsuccessful expeditions to find the wreck. Chalmers contacted Carey, took him to the wreck site, and dove with him to explore it. It is now a protected heritage site.

A few years earlier, in July, 1986 divers Wayne Brusate, Gary Biniecki, and Jon Severance used sonar to find another big freighter, the *Regina*, in the southern part of Lake Huron. Brusate, the first diver on the wreck, identified her by finding the ship's brass bell. The hull was almost overturned and it was surrounded by wreckage. For six months, the divers surveyed the wreck, finding no sign that she had been in a collision. Her rudder was set hard to starboard and the cladburn in the bridge, the mechanism the captain used to set the engine speed, registered "All Stop." Most of the cargo of pipe that had been stacked on her decks was gone, probably jettisoned during the storm. Around the wreck lay cases of canned food, cargo from inside the ship's hold. The divers believe the *Regina* was abandoned. That would explain why the engine was stopped. They know that the engine room sailors succeeded in launching a lifeboat because the boat that washed up at Point Franks held the people who worked below deck. The captain went down with the ship, and his body came ashore across the lake at Sanilac, Michigan in 1914.

One mystery remains. Why did sailors from the *Regina* and the *Charles S. Price*, another big freighter, come ashore wearing lifebelts from each other's ships? The divers believe the *Charles S. Price* entered the Regina's wreckage field soon after the Regina sank and tried to rescue the men in the lifeboat. When the Price turned to pick them up, she was caught in troughs of the waves and capsized about forty miles from the place where the Regina went down. According to their theory, the men in the Regina's lifeboat were thrown life preservers by their would-be rescuers on the *Price*. Later, they may have tried to save *Price* crewmen by helping them into their lifeboat and throwing them *Regina* life preservers. Perhaps crewmen on the *Price* had gone into the water in the wreckage field of the *Regina* and had found some of her life jackets to wear. Or was the storm even more cruel, allowing some of the crew of the *Price* to be rescued by the *Regina* only to lose their lives when the second ship went under the mountainous black waves?

Another theory holds that the life jackets were switched after the bodies came ashore by looters who plundered the bodies, but there's no logical reason for them to have done this.

The first bodies started coming ashore, in the aftermath of the Great Storm, at Grand Bend, Ontario. This was the day a "mystery ship" was found floating upside-down at the south end of the lake. Searchers found the corpse of a man wearing a life jacket from the freighter *Wexford*. He was frozen in a grotesque position, as though he were pleading for help. Two of his fellow crewmen were found the same day. The local coroner presciently set up a morgue in a hardware store in the nearby village of Thedford and waited as the lake began to give up its grim fall harvest. The next influx of wreckage came from the *James Carruthers*, the longest and newest ship on the Great Lakes, on her third voyage. The hardware store was soon filled with bodies wrapped in newspapers, so two warehouses were pressed into service.

Ten frozen bodies washed up on the Canadian shore on November 11. Seven wore life jackets stenciled with the name *Charles S. Price*. Three wore life jackets from the *Regina*. The same day, two bodies in a lifeboat were found. The lifeboat and oars were stenciled with the name *Regina*. On Wednesday, a lifeboat carrying eight frozen corpses rolled ashore at Port Franks.

By Thursday, November 14, the entire southeastern shore of Lake Huron was littered with bodies and wreckage coming from the *Price, James Carruthers, Regina, Wexford, Argus*, and *Turret King*, all lost with their crews.

Ghouls from nearby towns and farms made money by going through the pockets of the dead men, taking their season's earnings. Many of the bodies were never identified. The thefts made it harder for investigators to piece together the story of the catastrophe. On November 13, four patrols of armed men were dispatched to stop the looting and to search the countryside near the Lake Huron shore for stashes of wreckage stolen for its scrap value.

Some people had a lucky break. On November 9 the lake freighter *Matao* left Sarnia, headed for Fort William. Once the ship entered Lake Huron, thirty-foot-high waves poured over its deck, and the boiler room began to fill with water. The firemen worked fiercely, knowing the ship's survival depended on their ability to shovel coal into the furnaces. Captain Hugh McLeod managed to turn the ship around without losing her in the troughs of the waves. He raced toward shore, hoping he could ground the ship before her engines failed and she went under. Finally, at Port aux Basques, Michigan, the crew felt the welcome shudder of the ship plowing onto the rocky shore. The crew couldn't see the land, but they knew it was there. They stayed on the ship until the storm was over. When Lake Huron finally calmed, the *Matao* was more than 300 yards inland. It took more than a year to get her back to the lake.

The most convincing estimates place the loss of life on Lake Huron at 178 sailors. Overall, the death toll on the Great Lakes reached 248. The estimated value of the lost ships and cargo was $3,500,000 in the money of the time—probably fifty times that in today's currency. Many of the lost vessels were not insured or carried policies for far less than their real value. The sailors weren't covered at all, unless they paid high premiums for private insurance. Their families were left either to fend for themselves or rely on charities.

When telegraph and telephone lines were restored, about four days later, they carried news of a virtually unprecedented catastrophe across the continent. They told, of course, of the pride of the Great Lakes fleet having been lost. But there were also stories of people freezing to death on farms, stranded on drifted-in country roads with no one to rescue them, or trapped in the wilderness by house-high drifts. It took nearly a week just to clear snow off the railway lines, the main land link in southern Ontario. The railways were re-opened and the trains started running just in time to carry corpses of dead sailors from the makeshift morgues in the small towns along Lake Huron to their families in the ports along both sides of the Great Lakes.

In Goderich, which lost so many of her men, the parishioners of Knox Presbyterian Church hold a service every year for the mariners of the Great Lakes. A plaque in a small park at the west end of Cabot Street commemorates the storm and the people who lost their lives. A monument in the United Church cemetery, not far away, receives few visitors. A grave holds the bodies of several men who were washed ashore nearby. No relatives claimed them and they weren't identified. A fine granite tombstone marks their grave. It is inscribed with just one word: "Sailors."

Some sailors who had the misfortune of being mauled by the Great Storm of 1913 found themselves, twenty-seven years later, re-living the nightmare. The Armistice Day Storm of November 11, 1940 was, according to meteorologists and sailors, at least as vicious as the 1913 storm. In all, the storm claimed five vessels and sixty-six lives, all of them on Lake Michigan.

After a warm morning, the winds struck suddenly from the southwest and were accompanied by drenching rain which later changed to snow as the temperature plummeted. The winds reached peak speeds of seventy-five miles an hour, hurricane strength. The Pere Marquette car ferry *City of Flint 32* tried to make port, but was cast up by the waves about 300 yards from the shore.

Des Moines, Iowa was the first city to take a direct hit. By the time the storm reached Lake Michigan, it had already done most of its killing: some 110 duck hunters who had gone out into the woods of Minnesota and Wisconsin to take advantage of the abnormally warm holiday weather froze to death. They had left home in fall jackets and rubber boots, poor protection against that night's sub-zero temperatures and howling winds. Snowdrifts that grew to twenty feet stopped them from finding shelter. The Minnesota State Climatology Office rated the November 11, 1940 snowstorm as the number two weather event of the twentieth century. Only, the 1930s' dust bowl outranked it.

The *Edmund Fitzgerald* was the last and most famous ship to succumb to the Witch of November. (Those who are superstitious may want to knock on wood.)

When the *Edmund Fitzgerald* was launched in 1958, she was—at 729 feet—the largest ship on the Great Lakes. Her seventeen-year career on the lakes was uneventful. There were a couple of minor mishaps, as there are likely to be in the life of any ship, but no accident had delayed her for more than a few days. Ernie McSorley, her skipper, was born in Ogdensburg, New York. During the Depression, he signed up as an eighteen-year-old deckhand, steadily rising through the ranks until he became, at thirty-seven, the youngest captain on the Great Lakes. By the fall of 1975, he had been the ship's master for just over three years. He was due to retire in 1978.

On the afternoon of Sunday, November 9, 1975, the *Fitzgerald* left the Burlington Northern Railroad dock in Superior, Wisconsin, at the extreme southwestern end of Lake Superior. She was loaded with just over 26,000 tons of taconite pellets, semi-refined iron ore mined in Minnesota and shipped to the steel mills of Indiana, Michigan, and Ohio. Her destination was a steel mill in Detroit, just a few miles from where she was built.

When she got under way, McSorley and the members of the crew knew that a gale was moving toward Lake Superior from the southwestern States. The National Weather Service issued a gale warning for all the Great Lakes on Sunday night at 7:00 P.M. By then, the *Edmund Fitzgerald* was steaming up the Minnesota shore of Lake Superior in the company of the *Arthur M. Anderson*, another ore freighter.

At about 2:00 A.M., McSorley and Jesse Cooper, the

captain of the *Anderson*, talked by radio telephone. They decided the storm was dangerous and that they should take the northern shipping route used during the fall storm season in the lee of Superior's north shore. During that Sunday night, the two ships traveled parallel to Lake Superior's Canadian shore, past Thunder Bay, Nipigon, and Schreiber. They were too far from shore to be seen. By then, the weather service had upgraded the gale to a full-fledged storm, with the potential for fifty-knot winds. Early Monday, a camper on the southern coast of the Slate Islands, off Terrace Bay, saw the *Fitzgerald* and *Anderson* pass by.

The winds were beginning to increase, but weren't yet gale-force. In the twilight, they cleared the last haven before reaching the Soo: Michipicoten Island and the harbor it embraces. Then they turned almost due south toward the St. Mary's River. Throughout the trip, the *Fitzgerald*, the faster of the two ships, steadily pulled in front of the *Anderson*. Around noon, the winds were about thirty-five knots from the northeast, but they had begun to die down. McSorley knew the calm was the prelude to a wind shift.

Off Michipicoten, the *Fitzgerald* signaled the first signs of trouble. The waves were still less than ten feet high and the winds were nearly calm, but McSorley reported to Cooper that his ship was "rolling some." An hour south of Michipicoten Island, McSorley asked the *Anderson's* captain to help him navigate, because the *Fitzgerald's* radar wasn't working. The failure of the radar probably contributed as much to the loss of the *Fitzgerald* as any other single factor. Without it, the crew had no way of tracking the shoreline and being sure of their position. Lacking both depth finder and radar, the ship was practically blind, navigating only by compass. By then, winds were still about thirty-five knots. A heavy snow had begun to fall.

At Caribou Island, about eighteen miles from the entrance to Whitefish Bay, the *Anderson* stayed far from shore while the *Fitzgerald* sailed toward the lee of the island. The snow and darkness kept the officers on the *Anderson's* bridge from seeing the *Fitzgerald*. Both ships planned to sail between Caribou Island and the Canadian shore. Cooper steered a little to the east to miss Six Fathom Shoal, but later reported that the *Fitzgerald* didn't make that course correction. On the *Anderson's* bridge, Caribou Island and the *Fitzgerald* appeared on the radar screen simultaneously. The *Anderson's* bridge crew knew that the *Fitzgerald* could have been slammed onto Six Fathom Shoal. A few minutes later, McSorley radioed the *Anderson* to say *Fitzgerald* had developed a list.

McSorley's ship also had lost part of its deck rail and two of the covers of the ballast tank vents, possibly torn off by the wind. For the first time, McSorley seemed worried about the fate of his ship. He cut his speed so the *Anderson* could catch up, and turned on both of the *Fitzgerald's* huge ballast pumps. By then, waves were building quickly, high enough to roll over the decks of both ships. Cooper later said the waves were ten to twelve feet high. The force of the pounding water crumpled several of the *Anderson's* lifeboats.

The two freighters were steering directly for the center of the low pressure area. There is no evidence that anyone on either ship's bridge thought the *Fitzgerald* was in danger of sinking, but Cooper says there was a trace of fear in McSorley's voice when he radioed with the report of the damage to his ship.

Just after the *Anderson's* first officer reported in his log the *Fitzgerald's* damage, the U.S. Coast Guard issued a warning that the Soo locks were closed because of high water. The center of the storm was moving just south of Sault Ste. Marie, into northern Georgian Bay, and the best protection for the ships was in the lee of the American shore at Whitefish Bay. Already, several lake freighters and ocean ships were anchored there, waiting out the storm.

At 6:00 P.M., half an hour after nightfall, the waves had risen to nearly thirty feet. McSorley ordered his crew not to go on deck. The *Anderson* and *Fitzgerald* were now in dangerous waters. Cooper left the bridge of his ship. An hour later, the *Anderson* called the *Fitzgerald* with some navigational information. Then, ten minutes later, this conversation occurred:

Anderson (First Mate): There is a target nineteen miles ahead of us, so the target is nine miles on ahead.
Fitzgerald (McSorley): Well, am I going to clear?
Anderson: Yes. He is going to pass west of you
Fitzgerald: Well, fine.
Anderson: Oh, by the way, how are you making out with your problem?
Fitzgerald: We are holding our own.

Those were the last words that were transmitted from the *Edmund Fitzgerald.*

Cooper returned to the bridge just as the conversation was wrapping up, and noticed that the *Fitzgerald* was shown on radar to be about nine miles away, just approaching

Whitefish Point. The next time an *Anderson* bridge officer glanced at the radar, the *Fitzgerald* was gone.

As the *Anderson* entered Whitefish Bay, the storm let up. Crew members could see lights on shore and could make out some of the freighters that had taken shelter. The *Fitzgerald* wasn't among them.

The *Anderson*'s crew began searching the area around their ship with radar, but found nothing. They tried calling for the lost ship on different radio frequencies, but the *Fitzgerald* didn't answer. Then Cooper called the U.S. Coast Guard.

Testimony at the U.S. Coast Guard inquiry into the *Fitzgerald* sinking showed the crew of a lake freighter needs about ten minutes to launch a lifeboat in good weather, about thirty minutes in storm seas. The lack of a distress signal and the fact that bodies were never found strongly suggests the *Fitzgerald* went to the bottom before any crew members had a chance to move from their stations, if they were on duty, or their berths if they weren't.

Probably, when the ship began her dive, the crew of the *Fitzgerald* knew the ship was doomed, but there was no time to react. The bow of the boat plunged into the water first. Within seconds, it was far enough down that the pressure smashed every window, forcing water into the forward cabins, and drowning or crushing the men inside. The *Fitzgerald* was actually longer than the lake was deep at the place where she sank. Her bow, with the weight of the fully loaded ship behind her, hit the bottom within a few seconds.

As the *Fitzgerald*'s bow dug into the bottom, her stern rose above the waves. The ship tore in half about midway along her cargo deck and part of the hull disintegrated into a flutter of crumpled, torn steel plates that quickly plunged to the lake bottom. The stern of the *Fitzgerald* rolled as it fell toward the lake bottom and landed upside-down. It is likely the sailors in the stern died before they were crushed in the impact.

A Coast Guard survey of eastern Lake Superior at the end November located the *Fitzgerald*'s wreckage, and plans were made to photograph the ship the next spring. Remembrance services were held at the home ports of the ship's crew and at Detroit's old Maritime Sailors' Church, now nearly hidden by the skyscrapers along the river's shore. A haunting song by Canadian folk singer Gordon Lightfoot ignited the public's imagination about the Great Lakes' last big wreck, and people who had never seen the fury of a Great Lakes storm argued over the causes of the *Fitzgerald*'s sinking.

In the summer of 1995, the bell of the *Fitzgerald* was raised and placed on display in a memorial at Whitefish Point, Michigan. It was replaced on the wreck by a bell inscribed with the names of the lost crewmen, a fitting grave marker to the men who went down on one of the lakes' most famous ships.

And what of the Witch? As of this writing, it's been almost thirty years since the lakes claimed a full-sized freighter. Three generations ago, the loss of two or three in a year was considered normal. The waterways aren't as busy these days, the ships are safer, the communications and weather forecasting systems are better. But complacency is the bait that serves the Witch well.

CHAPTER THREE

Remember the *Caroline*

H ELL RAISERS, disturbers of the peace, rebels, traitors. Of course, sometimes they're called patriots,
freedom-fighters, visionaries. In their own time,
the Rebels of 1837 stirred the same emotions that terrorists
inspire today, but their cause was won long ago, and the
threat they posed has been forgotten.

Oddly, most of the action associated with the Upper
Canada Rebellion of 1837 happened in the year or two after
1837. The year, however, was eventful. Michigan was admitted to the union as the twenty-sixth state. (The state's first
governor would secretly give the Canadian rebels valuable
tips to keep them out of the hands of the U.S. and British
armies.) Andrew Jackson left office and Martin van Buren
moved into the White House. Queen Victoria, a plump but
attractive girl of eighteen, began her long reign. The telegraph was patented by Samuel Morse. The first electric

Francis Bond Head, war hero and best-selling author, was an exceptionally poor administrator.

printing press was patented. The British invented the postage stamp (but wouldn't begin using it for another four years). A financial panic on Wall Street wiped out the wealth of thousands of Americans.

That panic was part of a cycle that settled upon North America in the 1820s and 1830s. Recessions were very common during the nineteenth century. In the backwater of British North America, tough economic times drew attention to the lackluster government that presided, more or less corruptly, over the population. The ambitious and able governors who had been sent from England before the War of 1812 now were replaced by second-rate men—the British colonial office had concluded that Canada no longer merited the best and brightest administrators. The governor of Upper Canada, Francis Bond Head, was so plainly mediocre that, according to rumor, he had been sent because of an unfortunate mix-up: his more talented cousin, Edmund, was meant to get the job. And Edmund, in fact, became governor several years later.

Francis Bond Head was an engineer who had served in the British army in the Mediterranean. At twenty-three, he had seen action at the Battle of Waterloo, an achievement that opened many doors in British society and the civil service. In his thirties, he had traveled in South America, prospecting for gold and silver. In his spare time, he wrote travelogues that were popular in England. Back in the army, he tried (rather unsuccessfully) to instruct his men in the art of throwing the South American lasso. He wrote another two books in the early 1830s both of which became bestsellers. He was knighted and shipped out to Upper Canada in 1835. He was a soldier, adventurer, and a successful author. He had all of the skills of a great Victorian leader except one: he could not manage people, especially civilians. He did not like politicians. As the representative of the British Crown in Canada, he simply would not deal with them.

The rebel William Lyon Mackenzie accepted help from doubtful characters.

He found his Canadian nemesis in William Lyon Mackenzie. This local politician had several strikes against him in the British aristocrat's eyes: he was a Scot when Scots were considered by the English to be inferior. He was a small businessman, and consequently looked upon as a money-grubbing, bourgeois liberal. (He was not so liberal, however, that he was above crushing a printer's union that struck his printing plant). He was also a journalist and politician in a time when politicians and journalists were believed to fish for power in the gutter. Bond Head's power came from the Crown and the gentry of England, while Mackenzie's came from the farmer and the small business owner.

Some Canadian historians have tried to paint the fight between Bond Head and Mackenzie as a struggle between an arrogant and corrupt colonial official on the one hand, and a crusading democrat on the other. True, Bond Head was no advocate of democracy. He believed he, as the representative of a higher power, gave better government than the colonists could possibly give themselves. And he seems to have lacked the personal avarice of many colonial administrators. His local followers, mostly second-generation descendents of English settlers and Tories who fled the American Revolution, did not. They made sure they profited from all of the farmland sales in the province and got any government business that was available. They also ran the police, the courts, and the legislature with a firm hand.

Mackenzie advocated an American-style republic, one that valued initiative, enterprise, risk, and brains. Still, no one should project today's idea of public morality onto North American politics of the eighteenth century. Politics in the days before the secret ballot, the career civil service, and tendered government contracts, were sleazy, cynical, and amoral almost everywhere. Anyone who has lived in a small town might recognize the politics of Upper Canada as the typical struggle between the

entrenched power of old money—the old boy's network—
and ambitious people who have, for one reason or
another, found themselves on the outs.

Bond Head and his followers tried to keep Mackenzie
and his democratic reformers firmly in their place. Three
times, Bond Head had his local henchmen expel Mackenzie
from the colonial legislature. Hooligans employed by the
regime smashed up Mackenzie's printing shop and tossed
the press into Lake Ontario. In return, Mackenzie, through
his newspaper, heaped scorn on Bond Head, and exposed
the corruption among the small group of families who held
power in the province. Eventually, though, Bond Head
gained the upper hand, and the last option left to Mackenzie
and his supporters was armed rebellion.

In early December, 1837, they marched down Yonge
Street, the road north from Toronto, and tried to take that
town of 8,000 people. A short exchange of gunfire in the
area of Wellesley and Sherbourne streets (now the heart of
the city's downtown gay village) ended with a couple of dead
and the rout of Mackenzie's cohorts. Barely ahead of his cap-
tors—by one account he came within forty yards of being
captured by loyalist cavalry—he found his way to the
Niagara frontier. Supporters helped him evade British troops
and get across the Niagara River. On December 11, he was
warm and dry in Buffalo. Bond Head put a hefty reward on
his head and demanded New York hand Mackenzie over.

General Thomas Jefferson Sutherland and Colonel van
Rensellaer were among the first Americans to pledge their
money, weapons, and lives to the Canadian rebel cause.
Both men were frauds. While Sutherland had some military
experience, his major contribution to the campaign was

tough talk. He recruited openly in Buffalo, a city thick with British spies. Van Rensellaer was an even bigger fraud. His father was a famous Revolutionary War general, but the son was shiftless. He claimed to be a West Point graduate and an officer in South American liberator Simon Bolivar's revolutionary army—both lies.

The two Americans quickly took over the Canadian revolution. Mackenzie wanted to join a rebel force in rural Ontario, but the American leaders and their foot-soldiers packed him off to Navy Island just three days after his arrival in Buffalo. That small piece of land jutting from the rapids leading to the precipice of Niagara was a piece of British territory, and they wanted it back.

To give the enterprise a semblance of legitimacy, Mackenzie was installed as president and a provisional government was set up. Its first act was to issue a proclamation offering 300 acres of good farmland in Canada to anyone who joined the cause. A few months later, the pot was sweetened with the promise of $100 in cash. A flag with two stars, representing Upper and Lower Canada, was run up. The government bought a big official seal for its documents, and began issuing paper notes in one- and ten-dollar denominations. Merchants on both sides of the river made the sensible decision not to accept them. Van Rensellaer's next notable official act was to go on an extended pre-Christmas drunk.

By Christmas, more than 200 American and Canadian volunteers were crowded onto the island, waiting for something to do. Doctors and engineers offered their services. Military veterans trained the men. Guns, including a few small cannon, found their way to the Navy Island republic.

By the third week of December, twelve cannon fired balls and grapeshot into the village of Chippewa and the woods that sheltered the loyalist militia. No one was hit.

The rebels' most valuable possession was a small steamboat, the *Caroline*, leased to the rebels by William Wells of Buffalo. Wells made one stipulation: that the ship be insured against loss caused by an act either of God or man. Somehow, an insurer was found, Wells was paid, and the *Caroline* headed downriver to be the supply boat and navy of Mackenzie's government.

On December 28, the forty-five-ton steamer reached Navy Island and was put into service transporting men, food, and munitions. Colonel MacNab, head of the local militia and a future premier of the united provinces of Canada, had heard about the *Caroline*'s mission, and had sent men to shadow her. They had instructions to report on the number of passengers and the volume of freight taken to Navy Island. MacNab's men tried to hide in a small boat upriver of Navy Island, but they were quickly spotted, and had to dodge musket fire to get back to the Canadian shore. Their report convinced MacNab that he had to destroy the *Caroline*, and as quickly as possible.

On December 28, MacNab, a veteran of the War of 1812, put together a team of militiamen to storm the *Caroline* and burn her. At midnight, seven small boats carrying about fifty men under the command of a Captain Drew of the Royal Navy set out from Chippewa. They arrived within about twenty yards of the *Caroline* about a half-hour later. Rebel sentries spotted them and shouted an alarm to the *Caroline*'s crew. It was too late. The ship was taken within minutes. One rebel was killed, two loyalists

The sad, spectacular end of the Caroline.

were wounded, and the ship's crew and passengers, some thirty-three in all, were driven off the ship at sword-point. One of them was Wells, who limped along the shore until he was found by one of the Navy Island garrison.

Militia captain Richard Arnold set the ship on fire while the rest of the attackers cut her free of the pier. The little fleet of militia boats towed the *Caroline* into the current. About sixty feet from the pier, the militiamen set her loose, gave three cheers, and watched as the *Caroline* headed for the brink of the falls. The *Caroline* provided a spectacular, if brief, lightshow as she burned, broke on the rocks above the falls, and plunged over them.

The American government took a rather jaundiced view of the game being played at Niagara. Henry Clay, the fire-breather who had pushed the United States into the War of 1812, spoke in the United States Senate against Americans who joined the Canadian rebels. More than 2,000 New

York militiamen were sent to the Niagara frontier. Some may have sympathized with the Canadians but, by the spring of 1838, the republican experiment on Navy Island had come to an end. Van Rensaeller, Sutherland, and Mackenzie's men either drifted off to some other cause, or joined new rebel groups forming in Cleveland, Detroit, and in eastern New York.

The next move in this campaign was made by William Johnson, a pirate who scuttled back and forth across the boundary in the Thousand Islands area of the St. Lawrence River. Johnson, born at Trois Rivières, Quebec in 1793, carried a lifetime grudge against the British over a real or imagined insult during the War of 1812. For two decades, he and his nasty daughters controlled most of the smuggling in the Thousand Islands. He also had no qualms about preying on small boats, attacking them by stealth in a sort of freshwater highway robbery. Although he had never been slighted by Bond Head, and his followers and never met Mackenzie, the Rebellion of 1837 gave Johnson the chance to move up to the big leagues of marine larceny by pretending to be a patriot.

On May 29, 1838, Johnson led about forty men in a boarding party against the steamer *Sir Robert Peel*. The ship was captured near Wells' Island. Johnson and his men later claimed the attack was political—they had shouted "Remember the *Caroline!*" as they stormed aboard the *Sir Robert Peel*—but their actions imply that they were driven chiefly by the desire for profit. Disguised and in blackface, they roughed up the eighty passengers, robbing men and women alike. One man was relieved of $6,000, a fortune in those days. Some of the attackers pawed through the ship's cargo while others looted the bridge and robbed the officers. After dropping the passengers and crew on Wells' Island, they towed the vessel out into the river, set her on fire, and burned her to the waterline. Bond Head sent outraged messages to the American authorities, and people on both sides of the border believed England and the United States were on the verge of war. Over the course of the summer, however, diplomacy prevailed.

The following November, Johnson was in command of one of the schooners carrying members of the Hunters' Lodges as they launched their invasion of Canada. The Hunters were carried on the lightly-armed steamer *United States* and the two schooners *Charlotte*, of Toronto, and *Charlotte*, of Oswego, New York. Johnson commanded the second *Charlotte*.

"Hunters' Lodges" were clubs that were formed in northern U.S. cities to overthrow the British colonial administration in Canada, ostensibly to aid Mackenzie's rebels. The Canadian patriots' role in their schemes was vague. Mackenzie later claimed he was not consulted by the leaders of the lodges. Mackenzie's enemies claim he stoked the movement, hoping it would put him in power. The lodges seem to have quickly evolved from a political association to a sort of armed company involved in a hostile takeover bid. As "liberators," they expected to have bestowed upon them the fruits of victory: vast acreages for officers, large land grants for enlisted men. And the Hunters' Lodges were rather top-heavy with officers. In the

fall of 1838, after the many farmers in the lodges had har-
vested their crops, their military leader, the self-styled
"General" John Ward Birge, assembled his men at Sackets
Harbor, New York. He planned to sail down the St.
Lawrence River and capture Fort Wellington, which then
was under construction at the Canadian town of Prescott.
The idea was that cannons at the fort would be used to stop
traffic on the river, isolating the British towns to the west.
These then would fall easily to other Hunters' Lodges and
Canadian rebel forces. That was the idea.

The British, who had always been adept at running spy
rings in the United States, knew most of the details of the
plan. The local militia had been alerted along the St.
Lawrence River, and work gangs prepared Fort Wellington
for battle. In the early hours of November 12, two schooners
approached Prescott with the insurgent force. Hundreds
more invaders waited on the New York shore. The Hunters'
Lodge boats tried to dock at the Prescott wharf, but steered
for the open river when the town's customs inspector,
Alpheus Jones, sounded the militia's alarm.

The Canadian *Charlotte* ran aground on the shoals at
Windmill Point, on the Canadian side of the river, a mile
below Prescott. Birge, dismayed that his plan had come
unglued already, claimed to have become ill, and had himself rowed to safety on the New York shore. About 100 of his
men followed in whatever boats they could find. The rest of
the men, about 200 Hunters' Lodge soldiers, were abandoned to their fate.

That fate took the shape of the military steamship,
Experiment, which arrived at Prescott on the heels of the
Hunters' ships. Within hours, about 1,200 British regulars

Thousands of spectators lined the New York shore to witness Canada's Alamo—the Battle of the Windmill.

and local militia descended on Prescott either by boat or on foot. U.S. authorities across the river were also alerted, and Colonel Worth of the U.S. Army, the local military commander, impounded the Hunters' Lodge boats on the New York side of the river, and ordered them to be tied up at the pier at Ogdensburg. Johnson, who would have been a fine prize for the *Experiment*, knew he couldn't take the ship in a fair fight. He scoured Ogdensburg for liquor while his men cooled their heels on the pier.

Birge, willingly stuck on the New York side, gave up his command to Nils von Schultz. Von Schultz was creative about his background. The aristocratic "von" may have been an affectation. He may have been Dutch, and his name has been alternately spelled "van Schultz" and "van Shoultz." His claims to have been a graduate of Sweden's national military academy, a mercenary in Poland's violent and abortive rebellion against Russia in 1831, and veteran of the new

French Foreign Legion in Africa, are dubious. He was, how-ever, a courageous man, and, in the days and weeks to come, impressed even his enemies.

In many ways, the Battle of the Windmill was Canada's Alamo except, in the end, the American martyrs gave their lives for nothing. Von Schultz would have been wise to sur-render at the outset but, like the men massacred in the San Antonio mission two years earlier, he expected to be saved by the arrival of reinforcements. Unlike the Alamo, the men in the windmill had a supportive outside audience. Thousands of spectators lined the New York bank of the river and watched the show unfold.

Von Schultz made his headquarters in the impressive windmill on the point, a building with three-and-a-half-foot thick walls of stone that was impervious to cannon fire. Its sixty-foot height gave the windmill a commanding view of the battlefield. Narrow slit windows were safe firing posts for some of von Schultz's men. The rest were deployed in the stone buildings nearby and behind low stone walls on the borders of the field. Still, as long as the British controlled the river, there was no hope of victory.

Von Schultz clung to fantasies: that the U.S. Army would allow his reinforcements out of Ogdensburg, or would send regulars across and join him; that the local people would rebel and join his cause; and perhaps even the militia and regulars would flock to the Hunters' Lodge colors. Von Schultz was one of those unfortunate commanders who believed his own propaganda.

By the end of the first afternoon, three British steamships with a total of eleven guns patrolled the river. Von Schultz had only three small cannon. Reinforcements would not be coming unless the American Navy was prepared to fight this little fleet. The local people, most of them descended from Tory refugees from the American Revolution, had been on the front line of the war of 1812. Those who did not come with the militia stayed home with their doors barred and windows shuttered. The militia and British soldiers who did arrive at the windmill made it clear they were prepared to fight.

On the first day of fighting, von Schultz's force was driven back from the outbuildings and fences into the windmill. Each side lost thirteen soldiers. About sixty British-Canadian men were wounded. Von Schultz had twenty-eight wounded men in the windmill, and another twenty-eight had been captured by the British and were on their way to cells at Fort Henry in Kingston.

Just before dusk, the British forces pulled out and marched to the warmth and shelter offered by Prescott, leaving scouts behind to watch for any attempt at escape. For two days, Von Schultz's hungry, cold men waited in the windmill either for reinforcements or a British attack. They had no blankets, medical supplies, or food. The temperature hung at the freezing point while a steady drizzle turned to sleet. One insurgent used a board to help him swim across to Ogdensburg. He arrived with news of von Schultz's plight and begged the local authorities for help. Colonel Worth of the U.S. Army asked for a truce and tried to negotiate the withdrawal of von Schultz's men. When the British refused, Colonel Worth allowed the steamer *Paul Pry* to cross to Windmill Point. The *Pry* passed unchallenged because the British gunboats were in Prescott. Von Schultz should have marched his men out to the *Pry*, but he mistook the ship as the bearer of Hunters' Lodge reinforcements. When the British steamers returned from Prescott, the *Pry* fled back to U.S. waters. It's possible that the British wanted the *Pry* to succeed. It would have saved the colonial authorities from the diplomatic fallout of fighting and killing American citizens.

On Friday, November 16, four days after the Hunters first failed to take Prescott, the British assembled their forces to end the standoff at the windmill. There were now three gunboats and four armed steamers in the river, some 2,000 troops, and enough artillery to do serious damage to stone walls. Von Schultz could not reply with his own cannon: he had run out of ammunition on the first day. Before a shot was fired, von Schultz and Lieutenant-Colonel Dundas, commander of the British troops, met for a few minutes under a flag of truce. They quickly agreed to a one-hour ceasefire to bury the dead. Von Schultz offered to surrender his men if they would be treated as prisoners of war. Dundas refused. In the fading light of that bleak autumn afternoon, the boats on the river opened fired, followed soon by the two siege guns, which had been sited just 400 yards from the mill. By dusk, the windmill was beginning to show signs of cracking and, at nightfall, von Schultz's men finally bowed to the inevitable, and ran a white flag out a slit window. Their leader, in the adjacent farmhouse, held out a little longer with the ten men under his command, until the British set the building on fire.

A riot broke out as the Canadian militiamen attacked the surrendering Hunters. Believing the Americans had mutilated one of their officers, the militiamen beat the prisoners with rifle butts, sticks, and their fists, until British regulars broke up the fighting. In the melee, von Schultz and about ten of his men managed to escape into the woods. They were captured again later that night.

"General" Donald McLeod, a former Brockville, Ontario schoolteacher who had moved to the U.S. and become one of the Hunters' leaders, described the capture of von Schultz in his book, *A Brief Review of the Settlement of Upper Canada*, published in Cleveland, Ohio in 1841:

> At midnight, all but their heroic commander were taken. He took possession of the Windmill alone, and fired so incessantly that the enemy thought it was full of patriots. At length they rushed in, and he jumped in their midst. They instantly pounced upon him like a pack of bloodhounds; tore the clothes from his back; robbed him of his hat, watch, and vest. Thus terminated the most extraordinary engagement that ever took place on the continent of North America.

McLeod added: "The Canadian Orange Militia behaved with the same malignity which has always characterized them."

What McLeod failed to say was that the militiamen were right: Hunter soldiers had carved up one of their junior officers in the first day of fighting. As well, they supposedly had left in the windmill a list of local people who were to be executed once the Hunters took Prescott. Those names were familiar to many of the militiamen.

About ten Hunters were killed on the last day. Two British soldiers died from sniper fire from the windmill. People in Prescott saw 156 prisoners march through the gloomy, muddy streets of their town to Fort Wellington. The next day, gunboats shuttled them upriver to Kingston. One of the prisoners kept a record of that night:

> It was midnight when we arrived at Kingston. We were tied together in couples, Von Schultz at the head, a rope passing between us.... In this condition with a line of soldiers on each side, we were marched to Fort Henry, about one mile distant from the landing, the band playing Yankee Doodle. During this march we were subjected to the foulest abuse from the spectators, pelted with clubs, and spit upon with impunity. Our heroic leader was struck with a stake on the hip, which caused a lameness from which he never recovered.

Von Schultz's days as a soldier of fortune were at an end. He rejected the sound advice of his young counsel, Kingston lawyer John A. Macdonald, and pleaded guilty to charges of treason. He told the court martial that tried him under strict military rules that he was wrong in his belief that Canadians were oppressed by the British. He accepted full responsibility for what had happened at the windmill. In his last statement to the court, he praised the professionalism of the British troops:

> We may fairly say that we owe our lives to them, because, had they not protected us after we surrendered, the militia would surely have killed the greater number of us. The sheriff in whose keeping we are has treated us most kindly, and done everything in his power to better the situation in which we were thrown by the miserable

cowardice of General Birge, Bill Johnston, and their officers. If our prayers were heard, those base rascals would have been delivered over to the British government by our own; and we would then meet our own fate with perfect resignation.

Von Schultz went to the gallows in Fort Henry alone. He left in his will £400 for the support of the widows and orphans of Canadian militiamen who died at the Battle of the Windmill. Ten of his subordinates were hanged in the Kingston city jail. Three other Hunters had already died of their wounds, about thirty had managed to escape (probably because of the willful blindness of authorities at Fort Henry), and all of the men under twenty-one were pardoned and shipped back to the U.S. For eighty-two Americans captured at the Battle of The Windmill, however, the horrors of Van Diemen's Land beckoned.

They were shipped from Montreal, along with fifty-eight Lower Canada rebels, aboard the prison-ship *Buffalo*. Ten more Americans arrived on other ships routed through London. Of these prisoners, seventeen died in transit or were worked to death. The captives spent their first years as slave laborers in Tasmania and Australia, building roads and fortifications. They were paid a little money and, like most prisoners, eventually given "tickets of leave." These tickets allowed them the freedom to get jobs or set up farms in the colony, but restricted them from coming home. Most British prisoners gladly accepted the chance to make a new life in the colony. None, however, of the 1838 rebels decided to stay. Almost all the survivors were paroled within five years, and the last ones left Australia for the United States and Canada by 1850. They took a pass on the Australian gold rush, which gave many British ex-prisoners the kind of wealth the Hunters' Lodges had hoped for when they fomented rebellion in Canada.

Other people were also on the move: Francis Bond Head was quickly recalled when the British government realized that he was a part of the problem, not the solution, to the unrest in the Canadian colonies.

Two more little battles were fought at Pelée Island and Windsor, Ontario, before the rebellion finally died down. Within a decade, the British gave Canada self-government and a new generation of politicians led the country into confederation with the Maritime provinces. The last Hunters' Lodge meeting was in 1841, and the room where it was held, in Cleveland, was just half-full.

Mackenzie escaped the noose but was ruined politically and financially. He spent twelve years in the United States before he was pardoned in 1849. During his time in exile, his property was plundered or sold off for pennies on the dollar. When he fled Toronto, he left a printing business that was earning a very substantial $4,000 a year (laborers in the province were lucky to earn a dollar a day). His bookstore held 20,000 volumes. His newspaper was profitable. He had a substantial amount of money owed to him by customers, owned a house, his business premises downtown, his printing equipment, several city lots, a farm lot in Grey County, and money coming to him from an inheritance. Against that, he had debts of about $3,750. His creditors were extremely well-compensated for their loans, and much of his portable property was simply carried off by thieves.

Although Mackenzie had a ten-year return to politics and business in Toronto, he died broke in 1861. Bond Head outlived him by fourteen years and went on to publish a string of bestsellers.

Mackenzie's few remaining assets eventually found their way to his grandson, William Lyon Mackenzie King, who became Canada's longest-serving prime minister. King added to the holdings by inheriting a beautiful house in Ottawa's Sandy Hill district from his mentor, Prime Minister Sir Wilfrid Laurier, and bought several farms outside Ottawa that were cobbled together to make up the Kingsmere Estate, near Hull, Quebec. King left all of that property and his personal possessions to the Canadian people.

As for Johnson, the pirate, in the summer of 1838, between his attack on the *Sir Robert Peel* and his poor naval performance at the Battle of the Windmill, he was arrested on the New York side of the border and charged with piracy. Represented by two of rural New York's best lawyers, he defended himself by pulling from his baggage a proclamation that he had issued while he was on the run:

> To all whom it may concern.
>
> I, William Johnson, a natural born citizen of Upper Canada, certify that I hold a commission in the Patriot Service of Upper Canada as Commander-in-Chief of the naval forces and flotilla. I commanded the expedition that captured and destroyed the steamer *Sir Robert Peel*. My headquarters was on an island in the St. Lawrence. I yet hold possession of that station. I act under orders.

The object of my movements is the independence of the Canadas.

Signed this tenth day of June, in the year of our Lord one thousand eight hundred and thirty-eight.
WILLIAM JOHNSON

It was enough for an upstate New York jury to set him free. A contemporary American newspaper remarked, "good rope could be better employed." Johnson spent the next couple of years dodging the law in New York for various high and low crimes before receiving a presidential pardon in 1842, and retreating back into his old haunts in the Thousand Islands. He died in his bed in 1870.

CHAPTER FOUR

The

Atlantic

I T WAS A NIGHT for mistakes. One ship, whose captain was greedy for the profits to be made by carrying immigrants to the interior, overloaded his vessel grotesquely. Another, after a mid-lake collision, underestimated the damage that was done with tragic results. It was as if the Lake Erie fog had infected their brains.

In its day—she was launched in 1848—the *Atlantic* was one of the newest and most comfortable ships on the Great Lakes. She was about 240 feet in length—not particularly large—but she was fast. The *Atlantic* set several speed records on the lucrative Buffalo-Detroit run in the four years after she was launched at Newport, Michigan. Her cabin passengers, numbering about a 150 during the busy summer months, traveled in modest style. A full complement of cabin passengers was enough to make the *Atlantic* a commercial success for her owner, Eber Ward. But the flood of immigrants who needed transportation to the western parts of the lakes offered the *Atlantic*'s owner a windfall.

Certainly, it was a propitious time to have a passenger ship plying the lakes. In the middle of the nineteenth century, Europe was a good place to leave. Beginning in 1845, a series of crop failures, financial collapses, and revolutions sparked a wave of emigration to North America. Blight—a kind of mold—struck the Irish potato crop, destroying entire fields of potatoes and even ruining those that were in storage. It was first spotted on potatoes harvested on the Isle of Wight. Within weeks, entire counties lost their crops. Since most Irish families ate nothing but potatoes and scraps of meat, the country was devastated. Disease, famine's twin brother, cut down the weak and the hungry, the old and the very young. Ireland was a tenant society in which farm families lived on the produce from their potato plots and grew wheat to pay their rent. The failure of the potato crop meant the expulsion by landlords of millions of tenants who were either too weak or too ill to work in the fields. More than a million of Ireland's six million people left their country. Back home, a third of the remaining population died before the potato crops revived in 1850.

Grain and potato crops failed in parts of England and Europe as well. In 1847, the financial markets collapsed, and in the spring of 1848, revolutionaries in Paris overthrew the government of King Louis Philippe. The revolution spread to Austria, Italy, and Germany, with flare-ups in much of the rest of Europe. In most countries, the old order was soon, often brutally, restored. Karl Marx and Frederick Engels tried to inspire working people with their

Communist Manifesto, published in 1848, but their theories were no match for the repression that came in the wake of the failed revolutions. Some farmers and laborers decided their future was far from the troubles in the streets, in the booming heartland of America.

The holds of old ships that carried lumber from North America to Britain were jammed with Irish peasants on the return trip. Disease and starvation culled thousands of passengers on these coffin ships. When the Irish arrived in North America, thousands more died of cholera in quarantine camps.

Those immigrants who survived the crossing usually reached land at either Quebec City or New York. The healthy and smart ones kept going. New York was a warren of slums, ruled by gangs that stole what little the immigrants brought with them, before putting them to work in sweatshops at starvation wages. In Quebec, Irish immigrants were kept in quarantine in a vile, festering "hospital" at Grosse Isle, where more than 6,000 people died of typhoid fever. Nearly as many perished in another grim camp just outside of Montreal.

The lucky ones made it to the Great Lakes. In the 1840s, Buffalo was the jumping-off point for most immigrants heading west. There was still good, cheap land to be purchased in the heart of the continent. There was no rail link across the plains—that would come later—so the last leg of the journey was across the lakes. Steamers carried newcomers from Buffalo to Detroit or Chicago, where the better-off bought farms sight-unseen from land agents, and the poorer ones set out for the frontier, hoping to get hired as farm laborers. Within a couple of generations, most of these settlers prospered, and had all but erased from memory the horrors of the trip to the interior.

On the afternoon of August 19, 1852, the *Atlantic* left Buffalo on her regular run. Every cabin was occupied and about 250 Irish and European immigrants were crowded below her decks and scattered in the open air on the top decks. Captain J. Byron Pettey heard there was a large number of Norwegian immigrants waiting at Erie, Pennsylvania, for any ship that would take them west. They hoped to reach Detroit, then walk inland to the new farming areas that were opening up in the fertile forests of southern Michigan.

The *Atlantic* arrived at Erie in the dark and loaded just over half the Norwegians on board. About seventy lucky, but enraged, immigrants were left on the Erie dock. There was no way in which any more people could be jammed onto the overloaded ship, even by the lax safety standards of those times.

The ship's purser collected as much cash as he could. He didn't keep a list of passengers, so no one knows exactly how many there were on board, but the *Atlantic* left Erie with at least 600 people crowded on a ship that carried about 200 people comfortably. Baggage was stacked in huge piles all over the deck. People jammed the ship, looking for any place where they could stretch out. They ended up on narrow walkways, even sleeping on the hurricane deck that covered the bridge and on the roof of the *Atlantic*'s cabin. Eventually, as the ship entered the open waters of Lake Erie, her giant paddle wheel beating a steady rhythm, the people squeezed on board adjusted to the cramped conditions. They expected to be in Detroit the next afternoon.

At 2:00 A.M. that Friday, the *Atlantic* was still in the eastern end of Lake Erie, cruising along the busy steamer track near the centre of the lake. Her three-storey-high paddle wheel dug into the warm water, while her bow cut through the fog that had formed when the warm, moist air rising from the lake hit the cooler night air that had settled over it. Below deck, the steerage passengers were warm and dry, unlike the men crowded on the deck. Some immigrants slept on makeshift beds. Others tried to rest by sleeping on the trunks that were stacked all over the deck. Between the commotion made by all these people, the roar of the engine and wheel, and the smoke that sometimes drifted down from the *Atlantic*'s two smokestacks, the cabin passengers weren't getting much sleep either. On the bridge, the *Atlantic*'s officers squinted to see their way through the fog.

Coming the other way, the steamer *Ogdensburg* was blinded by the same banks of mist. She was a freighter heading toward Buffalo. The *Ogdensburg* was a propeller-driven ship about the same size as the *Atlantic*. She came toward the *Atlantic* from the passenger ship's left side. No one on either ship was aware of the other until the two ships collided.

The people crowded aboard the *Atlantic* felt the ship shudder when the *Ogdensburg* struck. The hull of the *Atlantic* offered little resistance to the freighter, which buried her bow into the *Atlantic*'s baggage room. The people on deck were horrified to see part of the *Ogdensburg*'s bridge towering over them. The whole scene was accompanied by the terrifying noise of ripping metal and snapping wood, the shouts of the half-panicked sailors, and the screams of frightened passengers.

At this point, no one on either ship had been hurt, and the *Ogdensburg* was almost undamaged. If people had stayed calm, taken stock of the situation, and used some sense, all of the people aboard the *Atlantic* would have survived. Instead of evacuating the *Atlantic*'s passengers to the *Ogdensburg*, however, the crews of both ships focused on the damage to their vessels. Once the *Ogdenburg*'s crew was sure their boat was still seaworthy, they put the engines in reverse and backed out of the punctured *Atlantic*.

Once free of the passenger steamer, the *Ogdensburg* resumed her course for Buffalo. She carried on, in fact, as if nothing serious had occurred at all. Good sense was not much in evidence on Lake Erie that night. The *Atlantic*'s engines were still working, the paddle wheel was turning, but water poured through the hole in her side. Later, the *Atlantic*'s officers claimed they were trying to run for shore, but nothing was done to alert passengers that the ship was in danger. Most had been reassured when they saw the *Ogdensburg* steam away. Within a few minutes, however, the water flowing below the *Atlantic*'s decks flooded into the boiler room and extinguished the fires. When the engines stopped in a cloud of smoke and steam, the passengers finally realized the danger.

Showing some rather primitive survival instincts, a mob of men on the *Atlantic*'s deck tried to launch a lifeboat from the ship's starboard side. The boat was so crowded and the men lowering it were so incompetent that the bow of the lifeboat was allowed to drop and the men inside tumbled into the lake. At about the same time, Captain Pettey stumbled into another lifeboat, and landed on his head. He staggered from the boat, suffering from a concussion, and sat out the rest of the night's terrors in a daze.

No one took the captain's place. The bow of the *Atlantic* settled into the calm waters of Lake Erie as the ship gradually began to sink. The fog was beginning to lift. The water was warm and still, and the night was placid, but the scene around the *Atlantic* was tumultuous. Mobs of people tried to get on deck from below. Others were jumping into the lake while clinging to pieces of baggage or diving overboard in hope of swimming to shore, about three miles away.

When the collision occurred, Erik Thorstad, a Norwegian immigrant who had boarded the *Atlantic* in Buffalo, was trying to sleep on his trunk on the *Atlantic's* deck. He had come a long way, across the Atlantic to Quebec City, and then by canal boat up the St. Lawrence River, across Lake Champlain, and through the Erie Canal.

Thorstad described what happened:

> Since it was already late in the evening and I felt sleepy, I opened my chest, took off my coat and laid it together with my money and my watch, in the chest. I took out my bedclothes, made me a bed on the chest, and lay down to sleep. But when it was about half past two o'clock in the morning I awoke with a heavy shock. Immediately suspecting that another boat had run into ours, I hastened up at once.

Since there was great confusion and fright among the passengers I asked several if our boat had been damaged. But I did not get any reassuring answer. I did not believe that there was any immediate danger, for the engines were still in motion.

I went up to the top deck, and then I was convinced at once that the steamer must have been damaged, for many people were lowering a boat with great haste. Many from the lowest deck got into the boat directly, and as the boat had taken in water on being lowered, it sank immediately and all were drowned.

Thereupon I went down to the second deck, hoping to find means of rescue. At that very moment, water rushed into the boat and the engines stopped. Then a pitiful cry arose.

The ship was listing heavily by now and the passengers' panic was peaking. In the midst of all this one of the *Atlantic*'s big smokestacks crashed down on the deck, injuring a few passengers and adding to the terror. A handful of people, including Thorstad and two companions, found safety in a second lifeboat, which drifted on the lake without any oars. Few people noticed that the ship had almost stopped sinking once her bow and midsection had gone under. The stern section of the *Atlantic* floated on a giant bubble of trapped air. There were roughly 250 passengers still on board the *Atlantic*. Their screams, added to the pitiful cries of the people in the water, drifted across the take. About two miles away, the *Ogdensburg* had stopped again to take stock of her damage. Once her engines were shut down, the crew of the *Ogdensburg* could hear the awful shrieks carried across the water. Finally, after a night of utter stupidity on their part, they realized the passenger ship was in trouble, and turned back toward the wreck.

Ten minutes later, they reached the half-submerged *Atlantic* with its crowd of frightened people clinging to the stern. The *Ogdensburg* pulled alongside, and its crew began helping people cross from one ship to the other. They tried to rescue the people in the water but, for at least 250 of them, the *Ogdensburg* had arrived too late. Their bodies disappeared into the depths, or mingled with the wreckage and baggage that floated around the doomed ship. A short time after the last passengers were taken from the *Atlantic,* the trapped air in the stern finally began to escape, and the *Atlantic* sank in about 150 of water off Long Point, on the Canadian side of the boundary.

After spending about an hour picking up survivors from among the debris, the *Ogdensburg* steamed toward Erie, Pennsylvania, the closest U.S. port.

In Erie, the enraged and grief-stricken survivors held a protest meeting to denounce the incompetence of the *Atlantic*'s captain. Little was done to recover the bodies or search for any of their belongings, although such steps might have eased the lot of the now penniless passengers. Nothing came of their protests. Within a few weeks, the immigrants left Erie to try to pick up the pieces of their lives somewhere else and the disaster faded from public memory.

The *Atlantic*, meanwhile, settled into the thick mud on the bottom of the lake. She was upright, undamaged except for the hole in her hull, and the cold water of the lake preserved her nearly intact. Over the course of the next century, about 100 other wrecks joined her at the bottom at the eastern end of the lake. Except for the terrible loss of life that makes the *Atlantic* the fifth-worst marine disaster on the Great Lakes, she was just another tragedy in a time when overloaded ships routinely plied both oceans and inland seas.

Because the *Atlantic* now rests in Canadian waters, Canadian courts were to play a part in deciding how or whether she would be subject to legal salvage operations. The issue eventually made her an important test case for shipwreck protection advocates.

If there was treasure on board the *Atlantic*, John Green would have liked to have known about it. Green was a Canadian-born diver who lost his health trying to salvage the *Atlantic* in the years just after she sank. He was twenty-six years old when the *Atlantic* went down.

Green was born in Montreal, but he and his family soon moved to the New York side of the St. Lawrence River. While still a schoolboy, he made his first commercial dive, recovering a box of soap bars and a clock that a thief had thrown into the Oswego River. As a teenager, he made money by salvaging freight that had spilled in Oswego harbor and hauling cannon and other weapons off a War of 1812 wreck. Before his mid-twenties, Green never dove with an air link to the surface: he just held his breath. In deeper, colder water, however, he sometimes wore a primitive wet-suit made of three old sweaters.

In the summer of 1852—the same summer that the *Atlantic* went down, Green was on board the paddle-wheeler

Oswego when it was rammed and sunk by the steamship *America*. Green had relatives on board the *Oswego*, so he spent weeks living on shore nearby, and swimming out to the wreck every day to try to recover their bodies. Commercial divers working on a nearby shipwreck met Green and liked him. They showed him how to dive with "armour": brass diving bells linked to the surface with a rubber hose.

That fall, Green was hired by American Express to try to salvage the *Atlantic*'s purser's safe and some money known to be in a nearby cabin. The expedition was a failure. On the first dive, just below the ninety-foot mark, the air pump broke. The people working the pumps quickly hauled Green back to the surface. He fixed the machine and went down again. On the second dive, he found himself inside the *Atlantic*'s upright smokestack. Again, the surface crew hauled him back up. The third time, he reached the *Atlantic*'s deck. As he felt his way around the ship, his air hose broke. Again, he was fished out. His employers decided that was enough and everyone went back to Buffalo.

In 1855, Green was back at the wreck site after some salvage work on other vessels and a stint in the Caribbean. This time he was on his own, without the backing of any company. His surface ship was an old schooner, the *Yorktown*. Eighteen people worked on his crew. On his first dive, he used a small submarine to reach the deck of the *Atlantic*, which was now covered with about eight inches of mud. After five days, he found the purser's cabin, where the safe was located. Green tied a line to the railing, just outside the cabin, and went up to the surface for a hearty lunch. In an hour or so, he was back down on the deck of the *Atlantic*, feeling around for the small safe and hauling it out a window onto the deck. Then he went back to the surface for a hook and rope to haul the safe to the surface.

As Green sat resting on the *Yorktown,* a horrible pain tore into his chest and he lost all feeling in the lower part of his body. He had a near-fatal case of the bends. The *Yorktown* set off immediately for Port Dover, Ontario, to get Green to a hospital. There was nothing the doctors could do, so they sent Green to a clinic in Buffalo. After five months, Green was able to move around with crutches. By the next summer, he could walk again, but only with great difficulty.

He went back to the *Atlantic* on July 1. When he reached the wreck site, he found his line to the purser's cabin was gone. Although he was in extreme pain, Green went down to the *Atlantic's* deck and found the safe was missing, too. So was the money in the cabin next door.

Back in Buffalo, another diver, Elliot Harrington and his crew were counting the money for which Green had risked his life. Harrington was an inventor who had taken the design of the diving bell and had improved on it, making it into a sort of diving suit. Harrington had heard about Green's calamity and had gone out to the wreck in June. Within a few days, he found the safe still lying on the deck where Green left it.

Like Green before him, Harrington had felt his way along the *Atlantic's* deck. Harrington had a steel bar in his hands that he used to smash open windows and doors. When he found the safe, he attached it to cables that were pulled by a steam engine aboard his salvage boat. The steam engine gave the safe a powerful tug and the strongbox went flying, dealing Harrington a glancing blow. Had the safe hit him straight on, it probably would have killed him. As it was, Harrington had to be hauled to the surface to recover. On the next dive, the strong box was reattached to the cables, and Harrington got out of the way. Soon the safe was brought to the surface and the lucky divers began dividing the swag. They let the newspapers know about their good fortune, and word of their luck reached interested officials of the American Express Company.

The $36,700 taken from the *Atlantic* was a fortune in a time when many people were happy to work for a dollar a day. American Express went to court, demanding its money. Eventually, the case was settled, with the money being split between the company and the salvagers. Each of the four people who worked on Harrington's project ended up with a little less than $2,000, enough money to buy a small ship or a good-sized farm in those days.

Later, Harrington worked for the Union in the Civil War. He tried to raise the *Merrimac*, the first Confederate ironclad, and salvaged ships that the South had sunk at the entrance to Charleston harbor. He explored the bottom of the Confederate naval fortifications at Charleston, walking on the ocean floor to find ways for Union ships to pass through the heavy chain barriers that the Confederates laid at strategic places. After the war, he became an inventor, but not a particularly successful one.

Neither Green nor Harrington lived to be old men. Green's case of the bends caused him to be an invalid for the rest of his life, while Harrington died of cancer in 1879, when he was fifty-five years old. After Harrington's salvage work, no one bothered to take more from the *Atlantic*. There were easier pickings for looters on wrecks in shallower water: bells, compasses, clocks, and other artifacts that could be pulled up from wrecks that are more accessible with snorkel and Scuba equipment. Most historians believe that the only money to be found aboard the ship is the immigrants' savings, much of which would have been paper money, now long gone, or coins scattered among the wreckage.

Meanwhile, the ownership of the *Atlantic* wreck went into a sort of limbo. The owners of the *Atlantic* and the Ogdensburg were engaged in a legal dispute over the cause of the wreck that went all the way to the U.S. Supreme Court. The Court found both ships to be at fault and declared the wreck to be a total loss. Eber Ward, the original owner, tried to auction off rights to the wreck, but there were no takers. Then, in 1867, the Western Wrecking Company was set up to salvage the ship, but it's unclear whether Ward ever signed over his rights to that company. The Western Wrecking Company abandoned its plan two years later, and in 1914, the State of Ohio revoked the company's charter.

The *Atlantic* wreck lay undisturbed until 1984, when Michael Lynn Fletcher, a diver headquartered in Port Dover, Ontario, relocated it. He surveyed and photographed the wreck and left a buoy above the site. It soon became a lure to other divers. The spread of zebra mussels into the lake helped them find it. Zebra mussels devoured the algae of the shallow lake's water, and the wreck, long hidden by the tiny aquatic plants suspended in the water, could now be seen from the surface on a calm day.

In the spring of 1991, California divers, operating under the name Mar-Dive, announced they had found the wreck of the *Atlantic*. They paid the state of Ohio $14,000 to revive the Western Wrecking Company, and applied in a California U.S. Circuit Court for an order confirming Mar-Dive's rights. Ontario, however, has a heritage law that prevents the looting of archaeological sites, including shipwrecks. Provincial officials said they would not allow the looting of the *Atlantic,* and announced they would prosecute Mar-Dive if artifacts were taken from the *Atlantic* without a license. As well, they said, the U.S. court had no jurisdiction over Canadian territory, even if that territory happens to be under Lake Erie's waters. Punishment under the Ontario Heritage Act can be as stiff as a $250,000 fine and a year in jail, but the law's real effectiveness comes from the power it gives Ontario's courts. Judges can order any salvage to stop and jail anyone who defies their order by handing down jail terms and fines for contempt of court.

The summer after the wreck was found, historical preservation and education officials in New York State and Pennsylvania came down on the side of the Ontario government. Oren Lehman, commissioner of the New York State office of Parks, Recreation and Historical Preservation, gave the beleaguered Ontario heritage workers a boost when he said: "The importance and need to protect both artifacts and historic sites, such as those on the *Atlantic,* are in no way diminished because they are buried beneath water rather than land. Uncontrolled commercial salvage of this site would unquestionably compromise the qualities which make it significant, and would deprive the citizens of both the United States and Canada of a unique source of information regarding our marine heritage."

His colleague, Thomas Sobol, New York's commissioner of education, said his department would not have granted an archaeological salvage license for the *Atlantic* if it had been in New York's water.

"Our heritage is not for sale," he said.

The dispute ended up in Ontario's divisional court, where Canada's best maritime lawyer, David Beard, argued that the ship belongs to the Ontario government under the ancient right of the kings of England to shipwrecks upon their shores and in their waterways. He convinced Justice Douglas Lissaman that this right had survived through Canada's colonial period, and the power to determine the fate of shipwrecks lies with Canada's provinces.

Judge Lissaman tossed out the California court order, saying, "the only connection that this case has with the United States District Court of California is the fact that California is the residence of the Mar-Dive Group." They, according to the judge's verdict, "deliberately set out to create, after the fact, a scenario whereby a District Court in the United States would assume jurisdiction" by offering the California court "a substantial amount of misleading information."

Fletcher, not the Mar-Dive team, was the real discoverer of the wreck, the judge ruled. If the "finder's keepers" rule existed, he would own the wreck. But, because it was stuck in the mud—Ontario's mud—it belonged to the Government of Ontario in Right of Her Majesty Queen Elizabeth II of the United Kingdom and Canada.

The legal fight over the *Atlantic* wreck's future is over. Mar-Dive had the right to appeal, but decided to cut its losses and hunt treasure wrecks in the Caribbean. Still the *Atlantic* is a draw for salvagers who don't observe legal niceties. They're drawn by stories in U.S. newspapers, especially in Los Angeles, that have hyped the *Atlantic* wreck as a gold-rich piece of Americana. Estimates were given to the press that there is more than $60 million in gold coins aboard the ship, and that the *Atlantic* is so miraculously preserved that it could be taken from the lake bottom and displayed across North America as a sort of mid-nineteenth-century time capsule. We know for sure that Erik Thorson's watch is still down there.

In 1991, Steve Morgan, head of Mar-Dive, told Los Angeles reporters the ship is a luxury liner, its spacious hull filled with 600 rich passengers, many of them packing gold-filled safes. These claims were picked up by the news wires and printed in newspapers across America. The artifacts that were displayed at the Los Angeles press conference told a different story. A Norwegian cheese box, some old shoes, an ordinary snuff box, and some crockery: they were the belongings of ordinary people who didn't have much in 1852 and who don't even have a grave now. An electronic detection system protects their resting place and the police, along with honest divers, watch over the site to ensure that these victims' property and the shiny parts of the boat that took them to the bottom will not be laid out on an auctioneer's table.

CHAPTER FIVE

The Wreck
of the
Lady Elgin

POLITICS CAN KILL. The most terrible disaster that ever occurred on the open water of the Great Lakes was the loss, with more than 400 passengers, of the steamer *Lady Elgin* on September 8, 1860. It happened largely because a politician insulted hundreds of loyal soldiers just before the outbreak of the Civil War.

At 252 feet in length and weighing 100 tons, the *Lady Elgin* was one of the largest passenger ships on the Great Lakes, and one of the fastest. A powerful steam engine drove two massive thirty-two-foot paddlewheels. She was built at Buffalo, New York, for Aaron Patchin and Gillman Appleby, partners in a local shipping firm. She was named after the wife of Canada's Governor-General.

The Lady Elgin *carried both passengers and freight on Lake Erie.*

The *Lady Elgin* comfortably carried 200 cabin passengers, 100 deck passengers, 43 crew, and 800 tons of freight. The cabins were spacious and quite luxurious. Most of the ship's business came from the Canadian Grand Trunk Railway, which used her to carry freight on Lake Erie and Huron until the railway was completed between Toronto and Sarnia.

But the *Lady Elgin* quickly earned a reputation as a hard-luck ship. On August 30, 1854, she was nearly lost after tearing a hole in her hull on a submerged rock outside Milwaukee. She was forced to run for Manitowoc, Wisconsin, where she sank at the dock a day later. Her next accident was more serious: caught in a June, 1858, gale on Lake Superior, she failed to reach the shelter of Copper

Harbor on Michigan's Keweenaw Peninsula. She was thrown onto rocks near the entrance to the port and so badly damaged that her insurers wrote her off. She was stranded on the rocks for a month and couldn't be refloated until more than $8,000 was spent on repairs to her hull. Just a month later she was aground again, this time at Au Sable Point, and needed another $1,400 worth of work to make her seaworthy. Finally, she was sold, this time to the Illinois firm of Gordon S. Hubbard & Co, which used her as an excursion ship between Chicago and Lake Superior. Her new owners hired John Wilson, of Chicago to be the ship's master.

The United States was on the verge of civil war and the people of the old Northwest were divided on whether to support the Union. Before the 1860 presidential election, some senior Wisconsin officials, including Republican governor Alexander Randall, wanted Wisconsin to leave the Union to protest the continued legality of slavery and the repressive and vile Fugitive Slave Act, which forced free states to hand over runaway slaves. The separatist threat would become irrelevant just a few months later with the election of Abraham Lincoln and the secession of the southern states.

Only a few other lawmakers were prepared to go as far as Randall. While slavery had few friends in the region, the Democrats, who were a strong political force, argued against Wisconsin succession and the use of the army to hold the country together. In that election summer, the state adjutant general surveyed all of Wisconsin's militia units to see how many soldiers would support Governor Randall's threat to secede. Most of the militiamen were new immigrants.

Milwaukee's four regiments, the German Green Jagers, the German Black Jagers, the Milwaukee Light Guard, and the Irish Union Guards of Milwaukee's Third Ward were, at best, ambivalent about threatening the unity of the country.

The Union Guards, commanded by Captain Garrett Barry, were loyal to the Union and militantly opposed to any unilateral action by Wisconsin. Barry considered secession an act of treason. The state government revoked Barry's commission and disbanded the regiment. His soldiers were ordered to turn in their weapons and uniforms and to stop training. The men were enraged. They believed they were victims of the anti-Irish racism prevalent at the time. Instead of bowing to Randall's order, they decided to reorganize as a private regiment. They issued a public plea for money and, among other fundraising efforts, organized an outing that combined politics and fun.

With the help of the local Democratic Party, they planned a trip to Chicago, where they would join a Democratic rally and hear a speech by Illinois Congressman and presidential candidate Stephen A. Douglas. He was one of the more moderate Democrats: when his platform subsequently was adopted at the Democratic National Convention in Charleston, representatives of the slave states walked out. The "Northern Democrats" moved the convention to Baltimore and nominated Douglas for president. In November, he was crushed by Abraham Lincoln and the united Republican Party.

The *Lady Elgin* left Milwaukee just after midnight on September 7, 1860, and arrived at Chicago at dawn. Most of the passengers dozed on the overcrowded decks during the trip, resting up for the fun that lay ahead. The Union Guards paraded down Chicago's main streets in the morning. After the parade broke up, the soldiers and their friends went on a tour of the city. In the early evening, they returned to Chicago's downtown for the party rally. Just before midnight, the crowd assembled at the city's harbor to re-board the *Lady Elgin*. Captain Jack Wilson hesitated to take them on at this point because he was worried about the weather. But there was nowhere in the city for the passengers to stay, no one had made plans for any kind of delay, and the Union Guards pressured Wilson to leave. He gave in and, at 11:30 P.M., the lines were cast and the *Lady Elgin* started pushing her prow through the building waves and wind.

The *Lady Elgin* cleared Chicago harbor at midnight on September 8, 1860. She was loaded with the members of the Union Guards, plus several of Milwaukee's top Democrats and some wealthy backers, including Colonel Lumsden, owner of the New Orleans *Picayune* newspaper, who was vacationing in the North. Herbert Ingram was another passenger. He was a member of Britain's Parliament, and proprietor of the *London Illustrated News*, one of the world's best-selling magazines. He and his fifteen-year-old son were traveling through the United States. They planned to visit Chicago, then head north to the Lake Superior wilderness, before taking a steamboat down the Mississippi to New Orleans.

The voyage was primarily a party rather than a political event. The regimental band began to play soon after the ship cleared the harbor. Couples danced on deck while a few people tried to get some sleep in the cabins. The party lasted well past midnight. At 2:00 A.M., even though rain driven by a cool north wind sprinkled the deck, people were still dancing and singing. The *Lady Elgin* was steaming south, about ten miles from shore off Waukegan, Wisconsin.

At about the same time, the two-masted schooner *Augusta*, heavily loaded with lumber, was heading out into the lake bound for Chicago. She was owned by George W. Bissell, of Detroit, and commanded by Captain Darius M. Malott, of the same city. Her captain took advantage of the north breeze, which was stiffening into a gale, by raising every one of the schooner's sails. She moved along at a good clip, estimated later at eleven knots. The *Augusta* had no lights, but there was no reason why her crew could not avoid the *Lady Elgin*. The passenger ship was brilliantly lit. Investigators later determined that the *Augusta*'s watch officer, her captain, and some sailors stood on deck and watched the steamer for more than twenty minutes.

Captain Malott decided to pass the slower ship on her left side. It was an illegal move, possibly made because the *Augusta* was carrying too much sail and was out of control. At the last minute, he changed his mind, and ordered his helmsman to change course, but the *Augusta*, sluggish with her heavy cargo, didn't respond the way he expected. The *Augusta* plowed into the side of the *Lady Elgin*. No one on the steamer knew the *Augusta* was even out there until the schooner pierced the *Lady Elgin*'s hull just behind her giant paddlewheel.

The *Lady Elgin* kept moving after the collision, dragging the much smaller *Augusta* with her. A moment later, the bow of the schooner ripped out of the *Lady Elgin*. It pried off the paddlewheel and hull planking in the process, and the *Lady Elgin* lurched forward for several hundred yards before finally stopping in the pitch darkness. Captain Malott of the

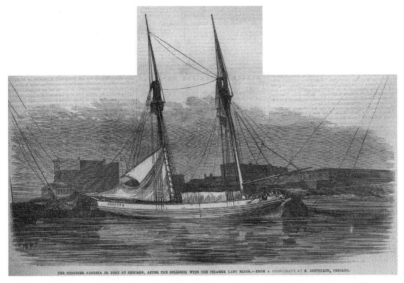

The schooner **Augusta**'s *illegal maneuver led to the collision with the* Lady Elgin.

Augusta and his crew were busy checking their ship over, making sure she wasn't holed. Malott told members of his crew: "That steamer sure got away from here in a hurry." He believed the *Lady Elgin* was only scratched, and that his own ship might founder. The *Augusta* then steered for Chicago, arriving there a couple of hours later.

Meanwhile, on board the *Lady Elgin*, Captain Wilson and First Mate George Davis had been asleep in their staterooms. When the collision occurred, they hurriedly put on their uniforms and headed to the deck. It was obvious the *Lady Elgin* would sink, but there was a chance the ship could be run aground. First Mate Davis rushed to the pilothouse and had the wheelsman change course toward the Illinois shore, but a few moments later, Captain Wilson came into the wheelhouse to tell Davis the *Elgin* couldn't possibly make it. The two officers and the wheelsman, George McKay, kept that information to themselves.

Very few of the *Lady Elgin*'s passengers were injured by the collision and the *Augusta* wasn't damaged at all. The *Lady Elgin*'s band stopped playing, most of her oil lights went out, and water began flowing through the wound in her hull. Fifty head of cattle carried in the ship's hold were driven out into the lake, and tons of freight were shifted to the right side of the ship, to try to raise the breach on the hull above the waterline. Survivors later said a dreadful hush came over the *Lady Elgin*. Some members of her crew tried to jam mattresses into the hole while others tried to calm the passengers. A few of the women put on life jackets while sailors and soldiers readied the lifeboats. Minutes later, several lifeboats were launched into the ten-foot waves without oars. The *Lady Elgin* slowly settled into the building surf while her passengers sought safety on her top decks.

The impact of the collision had cracked the *Lady Elgin*'s hull and, as the water poured in, the ship began to fall apart. Thirty minutes after the collision, the engine of the *Lady Elgin* tumbled out of her hull, and the ship slipped under the surface of Lake Michigan. The upper decks tore away from the sinking ship, and became a temporary raft thickly covered with passengers and crew. Even the faint hope provided by this refuge soon evaporated: the wave-washed hurricane deck broke into five fragments, each one still carrying passengers, who tried to stay on top or clung to the edges. Many of them, especially women and children, soon lost their hold and slipped away into the darkness.

There were thunderstorms in the vicinity and lightning periodically lit up the ghastly scene. For miles around, people struggled among the flotsam: pieces of the deck, a small part of the bow, some of the freight. The *Lady Elgin*'s captain rode one of these pieces of wreckage while carrying a baby in his arms. The child had been thrust into his hands by a drowning woman. He pleaded with the twenty-five passengers who were with him to keep still and not upset their fragile raft. Sometime in the night, the baby died, and he released it gently into the waves. Seven people, including the captain, made it through the night, and, when dawn broke, saw that they were among pieces of the wreck, bodies, and other makeshift rafts carrying both living and dead passengers of the *Lady Elgin*.

Fortunately, the water was warm. A month later, the lake would likely have claimed every person on the ship. One survivor who reached shore rode the carcass of one of the *Lady Elgin*'s jettisoned cows while another climbed onto the Union Guards' band's bass drum and rode the waves to shore. The steamer trunk that saved the life of another man is on display at the museum of the Wisconsin Marine Historical Society. Wheelsman George McKay, who couldn't swim, made it to shore on a bale of hay. Twenty-three years later, he and his crew drifted on Lake Huron for six days when his barge, the *William Trent*, was swamped in a storm. They came ashore near the Canadian port of Goderich. Whether he had good luck or was a "Jonah" who jinxed his ships was the subject of debate for years in many lake towns, but McKay himself, after several other close calls, believed he was the luckiest man on the lakes.

But even as the survivors drifted near shore, their chances of survival were diminished. Waves and the wind tumbled the rafts. Captain Wilson was drowned when his raft capsized in the breaking surf. His body came ashore three days later in Michigan City, Indiana. How could a man who was within shouting distance of the beach be carried so far away from it? A cruel trick of topography worked against the *Lady Elgin's* survivors. Along this stretch of the Lake Michigan shore, the beaches are narrow and the land quickly rises to about 100 feet. Large waves striking the shore roll up the banks, and the return flow of water creates a deadly undertow. Through the next six hours, people came ashore on wreckage, and more were drowned in the breakers or pulled back into the lake by the undertow. More than half of the people who made it to the shore were killed in those currents. Of the estimated 700 people who had sailed the previous night, at least 430 died.

The First Mate's lifeboat was the first to reach shore. It drifted in at the base of the bluff at Hubbard Woods. He climbed the cliff and woke the Gage family. One of the Gage boys was sent to the nearby railway station, where he woke up the telegraph operator. News of the disaster was sent to Chicago down the telegraph lines of the Chicago & Milwaukee railroad. Meanwhile, word had spread along the shore that a large vessel had been wrecked. Rescue crews set out from Evanston and other lakeside villages. The rescuers who worked along the five-mile stretch of shore where the *Lady Elgin's* survivors and corpses drifted in placed themselves in great danger: stepping into the water, even at knee depth, placed them at risk of being captured by the offshore current. Some rescuers from Northwestern University and the Garrett Biblical Institute in Evanston tied ropes around their waists and fought their way past the breaker lines to haul people in.

Edward Spencer, one of the theology students, was credited with saving at least fifteen, and perhaps eighteen, people. He spotted John Eviston and his wife drifting offshore on some of the wreckage of the wheelhouse. That scrap of wood tumbled in the surf, tossing Mrs. Eviston into the water. Her husband leapt into the breakers after her. He managed to grab onto his wife and began pulling her toward shore when a wave knocked him over and the undertow seized them both. Just as they were drawn back into the breakers, Spencer grabbed them and pulled them to shore.

The strain of the rescue operation nearly killed Spencer. He became delirious, screaming, "Did I do my best? Did I do my best?" and was said to have spent the rest of his life, as a minister in Rock Island, Illinois, in a wheelchair.

Others, of course, were drawn to the wreckage for reasons less noble than Edward Spencer's. For months, stories circulated along the Illinois coast of people who had robbed the bodies of the dead as they came ashore.

By noon, most of the survivors had reached land. The bodies took longer to arrive. Ingran, the British Member of Parliament, was washed ashore near Winnetka on the afternoon of the September 8. He was barely alive, and died before rescuers could treat him for hypothermia.

All through the fall, more bodies washed up along the southern and western edges of Lake Michigan. About 200 bodies were found altogether. Many were unrecognizable and many went unclaimed. Some of the unidentified victims were buried in Milwaukee under headstones in which the words "Lost on the *Lady Elgin*" were carved. Dozens more were buried in Winnetka in a mass grave. Like so many ships of that time, the *Lady Elgin* had no passenger list. The ship had left Chicago so quickly that some of those who did have tickets were left behind, while several Chicago revelers who partied on the *Lady Elgin*, but never bought tickets for the trip, found themselves heading for Milwaukee and the fatal rendezvous with the *Augusta*. Parts of the *Lady Elgin* came ashore in late 1860 and were taken apart for souvenirs. A large piece of her keel was used to construct an Evanston, Illinois, barn, which could still be seen in the 1990s. Other fragments and pieces of freight drifted on the lake for months before sinking or being salvaged and ending up in local museums. Some 1,000 children were believed to have been orphaned by the disaster, most of them in Milwaukee. Most soldiers in the Union Guards were Catholics. The loss of the *Lady Elgin* decimated the congregation of Milwaukee's St. John Cathedral, which continues to hold a memorial service for the *Lady Elgin* victims every September 8.

The loss of the *Lady Elgin* had political repercussions. Lincoln won the election, and enough Republican congressmen followed him to Washington to bring the secession issue to a head. Within months of the disaster, southern states began leaving the union. Governor Randall of Wisconsin was vilified for his political assault on the Union Guards. Wisconsin, at least in the early years of the Civil War, remained one of the most divided states in the North. To make matters worse, Randall invested much of the state's money in southern state bonds that were made worthless by the outcome of the Civil War.

The sinking of the *Lady Elgin*, the worst disaster on the lakes until the loss of the *Eastland* fifty-five years later, became the subject of dozens of paintings and lithographs, a number of popular songs, and a large local oral tradition. Stephen A. Douglas died the year after the *Lady Elgin* sank. The diminutive senator and political foe of Abraham Lincoln was buried on the shore of Lake Michigan, and, a few years later, an impressive monument was built at the grave. Before he died, he pleaded with the southern states to rejoin the Union, and campaigned among northern Democrats for support of Lincoln's commitment to restoring national unity.

Captain Malott and the crew of the *Augusta* came to a bad end. They heard about the fate of the *Lady Elgin* when they arrived in Chicago on the morning after the collision. But, rather than join in the rescue, he and his men went to the harbor authorities and tried to save their reputations. The *Lady Elgin's* lights were configured wrongly, they said. They thought they had just damaged some of the *Lady Elgin's* trim. They had just barely been able to save themselves. Their pleadings got a cold reception.

Malott was arrested and held for formal hearings that later cleared him of criminal wrongdoing. Sailors, however, considered the *Augusta* a jinxed ship. Someone on the Chicago waterfront tried to set her on fire, so the *Augusta's* name was quietly changed to the *Colonel Cook*. She stayed away from the Chicago area and was driven ashore and wrecked near Cleveland, Ohio in 1894.

The destruction of the *Lady Elgin* may literally have followed Malott to his grave. He and members of his crew, their reputations blackened by the disaster, found work on the bark *Mojave*. The *Mojave* disappeared without a trace almost four years to the day after the *Lady Elgin* disaster. All but one of the crew lost on the *Mojave* had been on the

Augusta when she rammed the *Lady Elgin*. Some people believe the *Mojave* went down in an isolated part of Lake Michigan, but rumors persist that her crew was lynched as punishment for the *Lady Elgin* disaster.

There is no single *Lady Elgin* wreck. Some cargo sank at the collision site. The ship's boiler lies on the lake bottom off Highland, Illinois, marking the spot where the *Lady Elgin's* hull broke apart. Other drifting wreckage, including the ship's bow with anchors attached, drifted for miles before finally sinking.

Divers began looking for the *Lady Elgin* wreckage in the 1970s when marine archaeologist Harry Zych launched a methodical search for her hull and debris field. In 1989, after about fifteen years of searching, Zych found the main wreck sites. He became embroiled in one of those expensive and long legal battles that spring up when salvors try to profit from their research. The Aetna insurance company had paid off the *Lady Elgin's* owners their $12,000 policy soon after the disaster and, in doing so, became the owner of the wreck. The company remains in business to this day and has never given up its claim to the ship. On the Great Lakes there is no such thing as a derelict: Ships either belong to insurance companies, some of which are either in business today or have been merged into larger companies, or they belong to the original owner and their heirs. (Warships on the lakes, like those in any other place on earth, are owned by their governments.) The State of Illinois, through the Illinois Historic Preservation Agency, also claimed ownership and wanted the wreck and artifacts left untouched on the lake bottom for archaeological study.

The lawyers were the last people to profit from the loss of

the *Lady Elgin*. Zych and Aetna reached an agreement that gave the wreck to the salvor. But the State of Illinois believed it had rights to the ship under shipwreck protection legislation passed in 1987. After a first round of trials and appeals, Zych made an out-of-court deal in 1993 with the Illinois Historic Preservation Agency. A year later, he changed his mind and asked a judge to vacate that agreement. The case went back to court for another trial and two more appeals before Zych, in 1996, was awarded the wreck. The state filed yet another appeal, which ended in 1999 with the confirmation of Zych's ownership by the Federal Court.

Soon afterwards, Zych realized that wrecks are more interesting when they're still in the water. Old timbers, hardware, and luggage has romance when it's part of a wreck. Dragged up and displayed on a dock, in a museum, or at a dive ship, most ship wreckage, no matter what ship it's taken from, looks like junk. People won't pay money to see the stuff on land, but divers will pump cash into a lakefront town to buy gear, hire boats, and pay for accommodation while they spend their vacations visiting famous wreck sites. Zych finally made the wise decision to leave most of the *Lady Elgin*'s wreckage in the lake.

It is now illegal in Illinois to remove artifacts from any Great Lakes shipwreck over fifty years old unless granted legal salvage rights, and all surrounding states and provinces enforce strict historic wreck conservation laws. A strong conservation ethic has also developed among Great Lakes divers, and those who remove anything from historic wreck sites for their own collection, or in the hope of making a profit, are treated as pariahs. Visitors to the *Lady Elgin* wreck must get permission from Zych and his foundation. That hasn't stopped unscrupulous divers from taking some of the more interesting pieces, such as Union Guards officers' swords, glassware, china, and even some coins from the *Lady Elgin*'s four main debris fields.

The loss of the *Lady Elgin* changed Milwaukee forever. Most of the city's Irish leaders perished in the disaster. Most of the few surviving Irish Union Guards members, joined by other young Irish men from the city, fought in the Civil War. The *Lady Elgin*'s foundering and the war took a heavy toll on the Irish. Captain Garrett's body washed ashore on November 8, 1860, just two days after Abraham Lincoln's election made Governor Randall's threats redundant. The Union Guards didn't have to travel to Chicago to make their voice heard. They could have proved their loyalty at Gettysburg and Shiloh.

CHAPTER SIX

The

Michigan

THIS IS A STORY of kings and pirates, of desperate rebels, and ships of war. And all of it happened in waters that are now the favorite cruising grounds of weekend sailors from Buffalo, Cleveland, Detroit, Milwaukee, and Chicago. The hero of this story is the iron-hulled warship *Michigan*, which, in more than a century on the lakes, was the main weapon used by the United States to quell crazed cult leaders, Confederate pirates, Fenian raiders, and many other odd characters who thought they could make trouble for the United States and Canadian governments.

The *Michigan*, the U.S. Navy's first iron-hulled warship, was built in pieces in Pittsburgh, and assembled at the Navy Yard in Erie, Pennsylvania, in the fall of 1843. She was commissioned on September 29, 1844, with Commander William Inman in command. And she had just one gun until the Civil War. She was built during one of those crises

that flared up between Britain and the United States periodically in the nineteenth century. The crisis blew over, the
British dropped out of this small naval race, and, despite
London's protests that she violated the Great lakes naval
agreement, which supposedly limited the number of warships, the *Michigan* survived as a relic of that troubled time.

Most Americans who knew of the *Michigan* would not
have expected her to be of much use after the British-
American standoff was resolved. Fifteen years after her
launch, however, she became part of the story of the bizarre
kingdom established on Beaver Island in northern Lake
Michigan. Today, Beaver Island is a quaint summer resort.
In the 1850s, it was at the edge of the Northwest Frontier.
A few settlers lived on the island, itself, but most of the people in the region had farms on the mainland or were loggers
based in Mackinaw.

The frontier had its share of people who did not fit in to
"civilized" society, so at first, people in northern Michigan
didn't take much notice of James Strang and his strange followers, when they arrived at Beaver Island in 1850.

Strang was born in New York State in 1813. He joined
the Baptist Church when he was twelve, but trained for a
career in law, rather than the ministry. He was admitted to
the bar in upstate New York, married, and settled into a
comfortable life as a lawyer, Baptist minister, and postmaster in Chatauqua County, New York. A few years later,
things turned grim. A change of administration cost Strang
his job as postmaster, and there wasn't much money to
be made practicing law in the tidy little community of
Chatauqua. So, in 1843, Strang struck out for the
Wisconsin frontier, taking with him his wife and three

young children. Strang's life changed the next year when he visited Nauvoo, Illinois, and met Joseph Smith, the founder of the Mormon Church. After a month with Smith, Strang converted to the Mormon faith. Smith saw potential in the man and made him an elder.

Smith had only three months to live. The founder of the Mormon Church was murdered in prison, where he was being held for destroying the office of a newspaper that had angered him. Strang claimed leadership of the fifteen-year-old church, saying he had been willed it by Smith. Strang's evidence for his claim was a letter from Smith postmarked a week before the assassination: "Nauvoo, June 19, 1844." The letter is in the collection of Yale University. The postmark and first page are considered authentic, but forensic analysis shows the second page is written on different paper stock, and probably a forgery. And this is the page with the text anointing Strang as the future prophet.

Brigham Young contested Strang's claim to be Smith's inheritor. He took control of the main group of Mormon converts and excommunicated Strang and his Strangites. Those who followed Young began the long trek that would take them to Utah. Strang's group moved to the less exotic frontier of Wisconsin, then on to Beaver Island for more privacy when an influx of non-Mormons settled in the region.

Strang was strict: there would be no polygamy, no meat-eating, and a complete ban on alcohol-consumption. He advocated a simple lifestyle with few material possessions. At first, his followers accepted Strang's dictates, and non-Mormons in the area tolerated them. However, when Strang used the colony's 700 votes to take political control of the Mackinaw area in local elections, and began enforcing his will on non-Mormons, resentment and resistance grew. And when he tried to strangle the whisky trade, the locals rebelled. The short-lived War on Whisky Point ended with a bloodless whiff of grapeshot fired from Strang's small cannon.

Strang was showing signs of mental instability. On July 8, 1850, he had himself proclaimed king of The Kingdom of God on Earth, though his real jurisdiction was limited to Beaver Island. He slapped taxs on the locals and strong-armed tithes out of local fishermen by having them dragged off into the forest and flogged. The money he collected was spent on a giant log church. Everyone on the island was forced to attend and to contribute 10 percent of their income to the church. Some of the money went to pay for a school and other civic works, but most was invested in sawmills and houses for the Mormons, and a publishing house that printed Strang's newspapers and increasingly bizarre religious tracts.

Things came to a head when Strang changed his mind and embraced polygamy. Cult leaders often drift into this sort of concubine collecting, though they never seem to advocate a reciprocal right for women. After he took two more wives, Strang's first wife left him and returned to Wisconsin. By 1855, Strang had five wives and had sired a dozen more children. Most other Mormon women had little enthusiasm for polygamy, and, despite the king's orders, very few men were able to get second wives into their cabins. Those who could not indulge in this sexual revolution could at least feast their eyes: Strang ordered all women in the colony to burn their skirts. They could be seen in public only in their undergarments. The tolerance of non-Mormon

Michigan settlers was stretched even further when King James began animal sacrifices. Livestock went up in smoke every July 8—King's Day.

Michigan officials had turned a blind eye to Strang, but word of his bizarre behavior reached Washington. Senator Stephen A. Douglas warned President Millard Fillmore in 1851 that the Strang kingdom was becoming a threat to order in the Northwest. Fillmore's administration ordered the U.S. district attorney in Michigan to prosecute Strang for offenses punishable in federal court, such as delaying the mail, cutting timber from public lands, tax irregularities, counterfeiting, and other federal crimes.

The *Michigan*, her deck gun loaded, sailed for Beaver Island. The ship carried a U.S. marshal and deputies and the district attorney who were to bring Strang and the other indicted Strangites to Detroit for trial. To prevent bloodshed, Strang's followers were lured to the ship by a ruse, and taken to Detroit where they disembarked in May, 1851. Nearly a hundred strong, they were marched up Woodward Avenue to the jail which stood at the corner of Gratiot and Farmer streets.

But Strang, a lawyer, was ready. All of the men were released on bail while the government tried to put together a case. In late June, the trial began, with Strang representing all of his followers. Strang demolished the prosecution, and, upon his return to Beaver Island, was elected to the Michigan legislature. While Strang rarely showed up, his elected status gave him much more political clout. He continued to make his own laws, meting out whippings for the slightest infractions.

While most of his followers accepted his rule and its

cruelty, the local fishermen and farmers remained restive. But the revolution that toppled him began with one of mankind's most basic conflicts: a dispute over an unfaithful spouse. In 1856, one of Strang's followers, David Brown, reported that he had found his wife in bed with his business partner, Thomas Bedford. A group of Strang's men seized Bedford and subjected him to seventy-nine lashes. Bedford then joined others opposed to his tyranny in plotting their revenge.

On June 16, 1856, the *Michigan* returned to Beaver Island. Bedford and one Alexander Wentworth led a group of forty men in ambushing Strang. Then they raced for the safety of the *Michigan* and escaped punishment for their crime. The gravely injured king was taken across to the Wisconsin mainland to his old home in the village of Voree. There, on King's Day, he died in the arms of his forgiving first wife.

Strang's followers were next to feel the wrath of the local population. Through the summer of 1856, about 1,500 Strang colonists were driven from Beaver Island, leaving behind their homes, farms, businesses, and anything they couldn't carry. In an orgy of looting and arson, fishermen and farmers from the Michigan mainland, backed by land speculators, stripped the island of everything valuable and divided up the farmland. Nothing survives of the colony except the name of the little village on Beaver Island: Jamestown. Some splinter groups of Strang's movement survive, but are scattered throughout the United States.

For the next five years, the *Michigan* had light duty on the Great Lakes and became a favorite training ship of Annapolis cadets. She earned the name "Mother-in-Law of the Navy" because so many rising young officers married Erie, Pennsylvania, girls. When the Civil War broke out, she was needed to provide an element of security to Great Lakes cities. Raids into the North were expected at any hour. Confederate saboteurs and their northern supporters, called "Copperheads," were believed to be lurking in the region's ports. In 1863, when riots erupted in New York City, the *Michigan* was dispatched to Detroit, a city with a large number of opponents of the Lincoln administration

On July 28, 1863, just weeks after the New York riots and the Union victories at Gettysburg and Vicksburg, Commander John C. Carter, the *Michigan*'s captain, reported from Detroit: "I found the people suffering under serious apprehensions of a riot. . . . The presence of the ship perhaps did something toward overawing the refractory, and certainly did much to allay the apprehensions of the excited, doubting people." During August the *Michigan* was called on for similar service at Buffalo, New York. In 1864, rumors of Confederate conspiracies in Canada again were rife. In March, Secretary of the Navy Gideon Welles ordered the *Michigan* "prepared for active service as soon as the ice will permit."

In the fall of 1864, the rumors of an impending Confederate attack finally proved true. On the morning of September 19, 1864, the steamer *Philo Parsons* was preparing to leave Detroit for a routine trip to Sandusky, Ohio, when two anxious men came aboard and asked Captain Atwood when the ship would be ready. He answered that his ship would cast off just after daylight. The men wanted to know if Atwood would take the *Parsons* up the river to Sandwich (now part of Windsor, Ontario) to pick up some extra passengers. The *Parsons* wasn't full, so Captain Atwood agreed to do so. At about 8:00 A.M., the steamer, carrying about thirty Americans and the two inquisitive men, drifted from her dock at the foot of B Street in Detroit, caught the river current and began making for the Canadian side of the river.

At Sandwich, four or five more men got on board. Then, at Fort Malden in Amherstburg, Ontario, about a dozen more people walked onto the ship's deck. They were scruffy-looking men, carrying a trunk tied with rope. Some of the Americans thought the men were draft dodgers trying to slip back into the United States, a rather common occurrence on the frontier during the Civil War. While they were tied up at Amherstburg, someone threw something off the ship. It was a note wrapped around a rock.

The suspicious-looking passengers on the *Parsons* were Confederate military agents. There was a double agent among the spies, a man in the pay of the Canadian government. This was not unusual for the South. Throughout the Civil War, the Confederate spy apparatus operating on the border with Canada was riddled with double, even triple agents, making it one of the great failures in the history of espionage.

Canada had a hard time with the Civil War. The British government was an obvious supporter of the South, but Canadians had stronger geographic and philosophical links with the North. Britain's policy was based on self-interest. Most of the cotton used in the textile factories of England came from the American South. The Confederacy was selling bales of cotton below cost and using the money to buy guns and ships from Britain. Slavery had few supporters in Britain, which had freed those in bondage in the empire in 1832, but the merchants and industrialists of Great Britain had control of the government, and the textile industry was Britain's most profitable industrial sector. As well, a division of the United States into two nations would have ensured British supremacy on the seas, and might well have made both new countries dependent on Britain for capital. The British government came perilously close to being dragged into the Civil War during the early years, but after the Battle of Gettysburg in 1863, the outcome was obvious, and Britain stood aside. Instead, the United Kingdom loudly proclaimed its neutrality while still paying low prices for its cotton and secretly helping the South with money and ships.

Canadians didn't import much cotton, nor was there much support in British North America for the cause of slavery. Many Canadians volunteered for the Union armies as a chance for a little excitement or to take a stand against the institution of forced servitude. Canada had a lucrative free-trade agreement with the United States that could (and, eventually, would) be cancelled if the Union government became angry with Canada. Authorities in Ottawa, the new Canadian capital, sensed the animosity toward Canada that was brewing in the northern states. As the war wound down, there were calls in the Union for an invasion of Canada as the last bit of work to complete U.S. Manifest Destiny.

Canada was just a few years away from Confederation and partial independence from Great Britain. It had its own legislature and civil service. And it had its own spies. Foreign policy was still, supposedly, in the hands of Great Britain, but the person who really ran Canada and its spies was the Attorney General, John A. Macdonald. The rock with the note on the Amherstburg dock was thrown there by a spy on Macdonald's payroll.

The *Parsons* steamed down the Detroit River and headed into Lake Erie. To the left, the spies on board could see the Canadian coast, with Point Pelée forming a line on the horizon. Ahead was an archipelago of flat limestone islands. Now they are the playground for prosperous residents of the Detroit–Windsor area, but in the 1860s they were as empty as that day in 1813 when Captain Barclay led the British fleet to its rendezvous with Commodore Perry at Put-in-Bay. Except for the graves of the British and American officers killed in that battle, the Bass Islands were uninhabited.

Except one. Johnson Island was a prison for 3,200 Confederate officers who had been shipped there to wait out the rest of the war. Most were Kentucky men who had been captured in Morgan's raid on Ohio. Only the presence of the *Michigan* kept the Confederates from leaving Johnson Island. By noon on that September day, the edge of the group of islands was within sight of the *Parsons*.

At their first stop in the islands, Captain Atwood left the *Parsons*. The first mate, a man named Campbell, was given the helm of the ship to finish a run that was supposed to be routine. The new commander, however, was getting worried about the scruffy passengers that had been picked up in Canada.

On deck, the strange group of passengers seemed a little more observant, a little more nervous, than the sort of people the crew of the *Parsons* was used to. When the islands first came in sight, one of the spies had asked Campbell to lend him a spyglass. In the ship's saloon, a group of regular passengers was playing cards. One of them muttered that the men indeed seemed like a strange bunch. Another card player noted to Campbell that some of the men seemed suspicious. The bulge of revolvers was apparent under some jackets. Campbell told the card players that he had noticed some of the men picked up in Canada talked like Southerners.

Campbell walked out of the saloon and went down below to check on the boat's engines. He looked into the women's lounge and saw a couple of the strange passengers loading revolvers. The mate was getting scared.

While Campbell was below, the ship stopped at its first American destination, Kelley's Island. The suspicious men seemed to be grouping into squads, Campbell noted, but their leader told them to calm down. They weren't at the right place yet, he whispered. The *Parsons* left Kelley's Island after a few minutes and headed for Cedar Point, now one of the more exclusive resort areas in Ohio.

Campbell was just poking his head up the ship's gangway after a check in the boiler room when a shot rang out and someone screamed. He saw one of the Southerners, armed with a pistol and an ax, chasing the *Parsons*'s stoker (the crew member who tossed logs into the ship's firebox).

"Go down below to the forward hatch, or I'll blow your brains out," the Confederate agent demanded. The stoker, however, got away, and ran to the bridge, where he hoped the ship's officers would protect him.

The spy then turned to Campbell and ordered him to go below and get the ship moving. Campbell just stood there

John Yates Beall

until the spy fired a shot between his legs. Fortunately, Campbell was a bit bowlegged, and the man had good aim.

Walter Ashley, the ship's pilot and co-owner, watched the action from the *Parsons*'s bridge. He later reported:

Five of the rebels were at the steps reaching to the lower decks, each armed with one or two revolvers and an ax.

The passengers and crew had been thrust forward on the deck known as the promenade deck, where they were being examined singly to see if they had any weapons, and after the examination, they were taken aft to the cabin. This was about XX? [*sic*] *o'clock*. After this part of the program was concluded, they were ordered down to the hold, excepting the ladies and children and a few elderly men, who were placed in the cabin.

The hijacked ship was then lightened. Much of the freight, including several large pieces of pig iron, was dumped onto the Cedar Point dock.

The men who captured the *Parsons* were a collection of amateur spies, soldiers of fortune, and scoundrels. John Yates Beall, a Virginian, was in charge of the operation. His second-in-command was a Scot, Bennett G. Burleigh, who was in it for the money. Burleigh had already been captured by the North on board a ship that had tried to run the Union blockade of Confederate ports. He had escaped from jail and found his way to Canada, where he joined Beall's raiding group.

To the passengers on board the *Parsons*, the leader of the spies was a man called "the Colonel" by his colleagues. He, rather than Beall or Burleigh, did most of the talking. The Colonel was told that the ship was running low on fuel. The closest place to get more was Put-in-Bay. The idea of heading to the site of Perry's victory in the War of 1812 wasn't appealing to the Colonel, so he talked with Beall and Burleigh, and then ordered the *Parsons* to Middle Bass Island. When they arrived, a couple of the rebels jumped off the boat and tied its lines to the dock.

Things started to go wrong for the Confederate adventurers. Four of the women hostages decided they had had enough of the war for one day, so they left the cabin, and jumped from the *Parsons's* deck to the dock. One of the hijackers fired three shots at the women, but none of them were hit. They kept walking.

At about the same time the little steamer, *Island Queen,* which supplied the settlers on the Bass Islands, appeared in the vicinity, steaming toward the island while the hijackers were still loading fuel. The Colonel told his men to look normal. Men in suits were rarely seen tossing firewood into the holds of lake boats, but the spies did their best to appear nonchalant. Their friends on the *Parsons* kept out of sight and told the hostages below deck to keep their mouths shut.

Three or four of the spies stayed at the front of the *Parsons* while the rest went to the cabin at the rear where the women, children, and elderly people were held. The *Island Queen,* with Captain Orr of Sandusky in command, coasted up to the dock. This part of the story should have been the end of it. The *Island Queen* had 300 federal troops aboard. These soldiers were on an unauthorized picnic to kill some time before being discharged in Toledo.

Captain Orr called over to the *Parsons* to ask why she hadn't finished her run to Sandusky, but he didn't get an answer. When he turned to resume work on his ship, the rebels at the front of the *Parsons* rushed toward the *Island Queen.* Captain Orr had no clue what was going on but he knew what trouble looked like. He rang his engine room to go ahead. The *Island Queen* didn't have much acceleration, however, and the rebels had little trouble catching up to it, rushing into the engine room and taking the crew hostage. It quickly became obvious that the 300-odd troops aboard the *Island Queen* weren't willing or ready to fight without guns. They did everything the eighteen rebels told them to do.

The size of the crowd of hostages was becoming ridiculous, so everyone was ordered onto the wharf. Some of the soldiers who were reluctant to leave their ship were smacked on the head with the blunt side of hatchet, but no one was seriously hurt. The non-commissioned officers, accepting their status as prisoners of war, promised the Confederates they and their men would not try to leave the island for twenty-four hours, nor would they fight against the Confederacy again. The spies threw a tow line to the *Island Queen*, and then left the Bass Islands in order to start, they hoped, the real battle. They hoisted the Confederate flag on the flagstaffs of their ships. It was the only time that the Stars and Bars fluttered over the Great Lakes on a Confederate vessel.

Elsewhere, the Canadian authorities were piecing the story together, while the bewildered crews of the two hijacked ships sailed Lake Erie, and the abandoned passengers sat on the Middle Bass Island dock waiting to be rescued. The government's agents knew that the Colonel was a Confederate named Johnson. They also knew that he was a double agent. He was the man who had thrown the note on the dock at Amherstburg.

The Canadian authorities realized the Confederates planned to hijack the *Michigan*, free the Confederate prisoners on Johnson Island, and take them on the *Michigan* and the *Parsons* to attack Buffalo, New York. The plotters intended that more than 20,000 other prisoners would be rescued from camps near Indianapolis, Indiana, and Columbus, Ohio. If the plan worked really well, rebels would be freed from prisoner-of-war camps in the Chicago area, too. They would attack the cities nearby, causing the Union to send troops north. Ohio provided 15 percent of the Union's soldiers, so the Union army could hardly ignore the assault. And if every hope nurtured by the plotters came true, then Abraham Lincoln would lose the presidency in the November election, and the North would sue for peace. Even if the war didn't end, pressure would be taken off the Confederacy, the thinking went, and there would be a chance the South could take the military offensive again. If all went well, a second front would be opened in the north, and perhaps Britain would be drawn into the war as a Confederate ally.

The whole operation was run out of Toronto by Colonel Jacob Thompson, a Southerner who had been secretary of the interior in the Buchanan administration. He arrived in Canada a few months before the Lake Erie raid, loaded with gold to buy guns and ships. He was an accredited diplomat, but he had secret orders from Confederate President Jefferson Davis: "Confiding special trust in your zeal, discretion, and patriotism, I hereby direct you to proceed at once to Canada, there to carry out such instructions as you have received from me verbally, in such manner as shall seem most likely to conduce to the furtherance of the interests of the Confederacy which have been entrusted to you." Basically, he had been told to make as much trouble as possible without blowing his cover and ending up on a Union gallows.

The Johnson Island plot depended on the skills of a con man in Sandusky, Ohio, named Charles H. Cole. Later,

Cole would claim to be a Confederate major, but he had never held a commission in any army. In fact, he had been cashiered from a Confederate regiment. Cole's motivation seems to have come from the $4,000 in gold that Thompson gave him.

Cole had been living with a prostitute at the West House Hotel in Sandusky where he posed, flamboyantly, as a wealthy oil speculator from Pennsylvania. Some of the $4,000 of Thompson's money was used to grease the social wheels in northern Ohio. Cole joined the Masons, and had, through the lodge, ingratiated himself with some of the officers of the *Michigan*. He cultivated a friendship with Ensign James Hunter and sent cases of whisky to the ship's crew. Possibly, if any of Cole's later dubious testimony can be believed, he had two cohorts among the *Michigan's* crew and ten spies in the guard on Johnson Island. On the night of September 19, 1864 he had an invitation for dinner. The timing of the hijacking of the two smaller ships was intended to coincide with Cole's dinner date and assumed that he would single-handedly capture the *Michigan* by slipping laudanum—a narcotic—into the captain's and officers' drinks.

Cole was ferried to the *Michigan* in one of the ship's boats according to plan, and the officers on the ship welcomed him aboard. Presently, he and the officers sat down to dinner. Meanwhile, the two captured ships dropped anchor within a few miles of Johnson Island. As darkness closed in, the hijackers waited for a light to appear on the bridge of the *Michigan*. This would be the signal that the officers had been knocked unconscious. So far, the plot was working.

The Canadian authorities, however, now had a pretty good idea what was going on, and they telegraphed the Union authorities in Sandusky with details of Johnson's message. The Canadian warning was relayed to Johnson Island and taken to the *Michigan* where the captain was called away from the dinner table so he could absorb the information. When he returned to the wardroom, he pulled a gun on Cole. Two armed soldiers quickly appeared to back him up.

On board the *Parsons*, Beall became worried. As the night wore on, no signal flashed from the *Michigan's* bridge, and there was no other sign to suggest that the plot was working. He began to pace the *Parsons's* bridge, wondering what to do. By midnight, he decided that the plot must have fallen apart. He panicked.

First, he scuttled the *Island Queen*. The hostages aboard that boat were brought onto the *Parsons*. The crew of the *Michigan*, still unaware that the *Parsons* and the *Island Queen* were held by rebels, watched as the *Island Queen* settled into about ten feet of water. As the ship went down, the Confederate agents could be seen loading everything of value, including a piano, from the *Island Queen* to the *Parsons*. The captain of the *Michigan*, already shaken by his dinner experience with Cole, ordered his boilers to be fired up. The *Parsons*, however, was already steaming toward Canada.

With the *Michigan* now a few miles behind and gathering speed, Campbell, the *Parsons's* mate, was ordered to steer for the mouth of the Detroit River and keep to the Canadian channel. It was becoming daylight when the spies reached Sandwich (now Windsor, Ontario). The Americans were ordered onto the dock while the Confederate agents ransacked their baggage for money and valuables. They tore apart suitcases and even carted off the stolen piano. After an hour or so of pilfering, the hijackers fled. While the spies searched for valuables, Beall chopped holes in the hull of the *Parsons*, sinking her in about ten feet of water. Until they began stealing, the men who hijacked the *Parsons* hadn't broken any laws in Canada. Now they risked robbery charges. Robbery was an offence that could leave them open to extradition and execution in the United States.

One of the first agents to be arrested was Burleigh. Canadian authorities picked him up within a couple of days of the raid and charged him with robbery. Union authorities filed extradition papers, causing a rift among Canadians, many of whom were Scots and therefore, perhaps, sympathetic to a countryman. Eventually, he was taken back to northern Ohio to face the charges. The jury couldn't reach a verdict. Sent back to jail to await a new trial, Burleigh escaped. He went back to Canada, but after the war he returned to the United States to work as a newspaper reporter in Houston. He spent the next fifty years as one of the world's most successful war correspondents, writing for Great Britain's largest newspapers under the name Bennett Burley.

Cole spent the rest of the war in jail, changing his story just about every time he was interrogated. His creativity has obscured the story of the Johnson Island raid—he left so many false or padded versions that it has been almost impossible for historians to piece the details together. After the Civil War ended, Cole was pardoned and allowed to resume his career as a con man. Whether he was a real spy, sincerely committed to the Confederate cause, or simply out for Thompson's $4,000 will probably remain a mystery.

Beall was the only one of the Johnson Island plotters to come to a bad end. The failure of the Lake Erie raid didn't deter him from making trouble at other places along the Canada–U.S. frontier. A month after the Johnson Island raid, he tried to lead an attack against Cleveland. This time, the raiders used small boats in their assault, but the winds were against them, and they couldn't get into the harbor. Two months later, he tried to derail an express train in Niagara Falls, New York, near the suspension bridge across the river. This time, the authorities caught him. He was tried for his various acts of terrorism and hanged at Governor's Island, New York, a few days before the end of the war.

After Lee's surrender, Thompson, the spymaster, tried to get to Halifax by traveling through Maine. On April 14, 1865, he was stopped on a Maine railway station platform, but not arrested. Someone very powerful had intervened. Abraham Lincoln deliberately allowed Thompson to escape. Politics is a small world. Lincoln had known and liked Thompson back in the 1850s, when Thompson was one of the most important men in Washington. The following day, Lincoln kept a date to see "My American Cousin" at Ford's Theatre. Thompson spent his last years, and the Confederate gold, cruising the Greek Islands with his young wife. He settled in a picturesque corner of England, where he died two decades after the war's end.

The real value of all the Confederate spying in Canada was in the propaganda it created for the Union. In the summer and fall of 1864, a tough presidential election campaign was under way. In August, Abraham Lincoln had expected to lose. In the same month that Beall and Cole were carrying out their Johnson Island scheme, the Democrats adopted an election platform that called for peace talks and the granting of Confederate independence. By the end of September, however, Atlanta fell to Sherman, the Confederates were driven out of the Shenandoah Valley, and the naval base of Mobile, Alabama, was in possession of the Union. The border raids strengthened the position of those who called the Confederates traitors and terrorists. Democrats in states along the Great Lakes who favored peace were silenced or arrested, newspapers were muzzled, and Republicans were elected.

The *Michigan*'s military service wasn't over. Some time after Lee's famous meeting with Grant, thousands of Fenians—fighters for Irish independence—gathered in Cleveland and Buffalo for an invasion of Canada. The militant wing of the Fenian movement believed Canada could be used as a bargaining chip for Irish independence. Throughout the war, the Union had made vague or cryptic statements implying support for the Fenians. Union recruiters had combed the Irish slums of Boston and New York for fresh cannon fodder, and agents were dispatched to Ireland to find volunteers, all on the assumption that the Irish had something to gain by assisting in the defeat of the Southern states. By war's end, one in five Union soldiers was Irish born, and many believed that the Civil War was also a struggle for Irish independence.

Of course, the implied support was something of a ruse, and in the months after the war, Fenian Civil War veterans had to fall back on their own resources. There were, however, thousands of dedicated members, most of whom had taken advantage of the government's offer to allow them to keep their military kit for a nominal fee.

Fortunately for the Canadian government, Macdonald's spies had no trouble infiltrating the Fenian movement. Word of plans for attacks on the Niagara Peninsula, the Lake Erie shore, and the region south of Montreal was relayed to the government, which called out militia units in Toronto, Hamilton, and Montreal. The attack was expected on St. Patrick's Day, 1866. When nothing happened, the militia was sent home. Two months later, Fenians won the last battle fought in Ontario.

On June 1, 1866 1,500 Fenians crossed the Niagara River just north of Fort Erie, Ontario, seized the town and took up strong positions in the surrounding countryside. Telegraph wires were cut and a feeble attempt was made to tear up railroad tracks. Their grand plan was to march about twenty miles across the Niagara Peninsula, capture the Welland Canal and then, with reinforcements, march another forty miles to sever the main rail line through southern Ontario. The scheme relied on thousands more Fenians following the advance guard.

They nailed this proclamation to trees in Fort Erie:

To the people of British America:
    We come among you as foes of British rule in
Ireland. We have taken up the sword to strike down the
oppressors' rod, to deliver Ireland from the tyrant, the
despoiler, the robber. We have registered our oaths upon
the alter of our country in the full view of heaven and
sent out our vows to the throne of Him who inspired

them. Then, looking about us for an enemy, we find him
here, here in your midst, where he is most vulnerable
and convenient to our strength.... We have no issue
with the people of these Provinces, and wish to have
none but the most friendly relations. Our weapons are
for the oppressors of Ireland. Our bows shall be directed
only against the power of England; her privileges alone
shall we invade, not yours. We do not propose to divest
you of a solitary right you now enjoy.... We are here neither as murderers, nor robbers, for plunder and
spoliation. We are here as the Irish army of liberation,
the friends of liberty against despotism, of democracy
against aristocracy, of people against their oppressors. In
a word, our war is with the armed powers of England,
not with the people, not with these Provinces. Against
England, upon land and sea, till Ireland is free.... To
Irishmen throughout these Provinces we appeal in the
name of seven centuries of British inequity and Irish misery and suffering, in the names of our murdered sires,
our desolate homes, our desecrated alters, our million of
famine graves, our insulted name and race—to stretch
forth the hand of brotherhood in the holy cause of
fatherland, and smite the tyrant where we can. We con-
jure you, our countrymen, who from misfortune
inflicted by the very tyranny you are serving, or from any
other cause, have been forced to enter the ranks of the
enemy, not to be willing instruments of your country's
death or degradation. No uniform, and surely not the
blood-dyed coat of England, can emancipate you from
the natural law that binds your allegiance to Ireland, to
liberty, to right, to justice. To the friends of Ireland, of

freedom, of humanity, of the people, we offer the olive branch of these and the honest grasp of friendship. Take it Irishmen, Frenchmen, American, take it all and trust it.... We wish to meet with friends; we are prepared to meet with enemies. We shall endeavor to merit the confidence of the former, and the latter can expect from us but the leniency of a determined though generous foe and the restraints and relations imposed by civilized warfare.

T. W. Sweeney.

Major General commanding the armies of Ireland

Sweeney didn't land with the first group of Fenians. This was a bad sign. Still, the Fenians had a fairly able commander in Colonel John O'Neill. He was to prove a much better field officer than his Canadian militia counterpart, Colonel Booker.

The first Canadian force to approach the Fenian positions was the Queen's Own Rifles, a unit made up of University of Toronto students and young middle-class Toronto men. They were joined at Port Colborne, the northern terminus of the Welland Canal, by the 13th Battalion of Hamilton. British regulars marching to the area from Welland would have given the Canadians a significant advantage, but the Canadian militia commanders and their men were looking for glory. In all, about 880 very inexperienced Canadian part-time soldiers, under the command of inept officers, left Port Colborne by train and arrived at the village of Ridgeway in the early hours of June 2. The train's whistle and the call of bugles awakened the Fenian pickets in the fields nearby. The bulk of O'Neill's men had arrived.

By dawn, the Fenians were deployed in strong natural positions along a low ridge and in the woods. Colonel Booker split his forces and sent them toward what he thought were the Fenian lines, but O'Neill had laid a trap by deploying several hundred men in an enfilade position in the woods along the path of the Canadian advance. Had that plan worked, the Canadians would have been slaughtered, but an over-eager Fenian tipped off the Canadians by firing his gun prematurely. The Canadians, now with something of an advantage, tried to outflank the Fenians, but a rumor spread that cavalry was approaching. Booker, falling back on tactics used in the Napoleonic Wars, tried to form his men into a square to resist the cavalry charge. Almost immediately, the Canadian officers realized that this was a mistake. Their men were in an uncontrolled mass at the intersection of two country roads and, had the Fenians charged, would have been slaughtered in the open. Booker ordered his men to form columns, but, instead, they ran back toward the village of Ridgeway. The field belonged to O'Neill. He had won the battle, but the war was lost.

The *Michigan* had prevented reinforcements from crossing the Niagara River. Generals Meade and Grant arrived in Buffalo on the morning of the battle and ordered American neutrality strictly enforced. Feints by Canadian landing parties in Fort Erie, and news that British regulars were moving up to attack the Fenian lines, caused O'Neill to lose heart. On July 3, his men began crossing back to the U.S. side of the river, leaving behind three of their own dead, ten dead Canadians, and about thirty-five wounded. The *Michigan* intercepted most of them and, by the evening of June 4, the scene on the Buffalo waterfront had turned into a carnival,

The Michigan *ended her days as a training ship for sailors and officers.*

with 400 Fenians riding around on a barge towed by the *Michigan*. While General Grant was unwilling to start a war with Britain by allowing Fenian reinforcements to join O'Neill, he also had no intention of causing harm to any of these men who had served so bravely under Union colors. O'Neill and a few of his senior officers were fined under the Neutrality Act and released to a celebratory crowd in Buffalo. His men were given a bit of pocket money and a one-way rail pass to the destination of their choice in the U.S.

Those Fenian prisoners who returned to Toronto with the bodies of the ten Canadian soldiers had a rough time. After being pelted with rotten vegetables by thousands of Torontonians who turned out to see them paraded through the city, most were sentenced to hang. None, however, actually went to the gallows. The last Fenian prisoners was pardoned in 1873 and sent back to the U.S.

For almost fifty years more, the *Michigan* cruised the lakes, mapping shoals and shorelines, looking for smugglers and reassuring people on both sides that law would be maintained. For a while, she was used to recruit sailors for the Spanish-American War. On June 17, 1905, she was renamed *Wolverine*, and her original name was transferred to a battleship. In World War I, she served as a training ship for sailors and officers. Finally, in 1923, her age caught up with her. The *Wolverine* broke a connecting rod in the Straits of Mackinaw and barely made it back into port. This was to be her last trip on her own steam. In the decades leading up to World War II, there were many attempts to preserve the *Michigan* as a museum, but America's first iron-hulled warship was sold for scrap in 1949. The money went to pay for the last tangible relic of the *Michigan*: a monument at Erie, Pennsylvania, crafted from the *Michigan*'s bow and cutwater.

CHAPTER SEVEN

Fire!

FIRE ABOARD SHIP is the sailor's worst fear. When a serious fire breaks out, the chain of command frequently breaks down. Crew and passengers faced with a grim choice between water and fire often panic. Sound design, skilled seamanship, and a reasonable amount of caution can protect a ship and its crew from most of what Nature can throw in their way. But fire is another matter. Fire haunted the lakes from the beginning of the age of steam. It took a grim toll through the years when the lakes were the main highway from the east to the Midwest. And it effectively ended the passenger trade on the lakes two generations ago.

Many of the worst fire disasters occurred on immigrant ships in the middle of the nineteenth century. The political and social unrest that began in Europe in the late 1840s, and culminated with the Great Famine in Ireland, created an

The Phoenix *was crammed with immigrants when she caught fire in 1847.*

unprecedented period of trans-Atlantic passenger traffic. Unscrupulous operators built ships in a hurry to exploit the business. Even after strict codes and better engineering made ships safer in later decades, especially on passenger ships, fire took a dreadful toll.

The boiler explosion on the steamer *Erie* in Cleveland harbor in 1842, which killed between sixty-five and 100 people, should have been a warning that many of the steam vessels on the lakes were death traps. The lesson was driven home on November 21, 1847, when fire broke out on board the *Phoenix*.

The *Phoenix* was a new ship, incorporating the latest in steam technology. At 140 feet, she was relatively small, but her screw propeller gave her speed and space advantages over much of the competition. Most of her trips were between the Erie Canal's Lake Erie terminus at Buffalo and the growing Midwest towns on Lake Michigan. The voyage of November 1847 was typical of her career. Most of her passengers that day were immigrants, Dutch evangelical Christians, who had faced growing persecution from authorities in their homeland. Nearly 300 of them had traveled to New York on the steamer *France*, passed through the Erie Canal to Buffalo, and booked passage on the *Phoenix* bound for northern Wisconsin. They carried their life savings in gold coin and looked forward to making a new home on the frontier of the Old Northwest. About seventy other passengers were Americans on their way west for the first time, or returning from trips to New York.

On November 11, the *Phoenix* began a slow journey westward from Buffalo, stopping anywhere along the lakes where passengers and freight might be found. At Fairport, Ohio, Captain G.B. Sweet suffered a bad fall on the dock and was taken to his cabin, where he remained incapacitated with a broken knee. The rest of the trip was miserable. Fall storms rattled the *Phoenix* all of the way up the lakes. Only Lake Michigan was relatively calm.

The *Phoenix* made for Manitowoc, Wisconsin, to drop off some freight and to allow the crew and passengers to stretch their legs. It was later alleged by some that members of the crew were drunk when they returned from shore, but there's very little evidence that what happened next was anything but an accident. Shortly after midnight, the *Phoenix* left Manitowoc, heading south.

Most of the steerage passengers either slept on deck or were jammed into third-class cabins. Captain Sweet was in his own cabin when a sailor spotted fire coming from the boiler room. Sweet ordered the ship's fire hoses to be turned on the blaze, but they did little to slow its spread. A hastily organized bucket brigade was also ineffective. The hoses did, however, extinguish the fire in the fireboxes, causing pressure in the boilers to drop, killing the pumps. As the fire spread through the *Phoenix's* superstructure, Captain Sweet and the first-class passengers took to the *Phoenix's* two small lifeboats. About forty people found seats on those boats. The rest were left to the fire and the lake.

Soon the entire ship was ablaze. Flames shot 200 feet into the air forming a great fiery arch. Men, women, and children crowded at the bow and stern of the ship, waited until the flames drew near before jumping into the frigid water. Some climbed the ship's mast, but it eventually collapsed into the fire. David Blish, a merchant from Southport, Wisconsin, could have left on the lifeboats, but stayed on board to try to save some of his fellow passengers. He helped to make rafts from doors and loose lumber, but almost no one, including Blish, survived by using the makeshift craft.

Chief Engineer M.W. House also stayed aboard to fight the fire and help the passengers but, when it became clear to him that no more could be done, he lowered himself onto a door in the water. House had the presence of mind to keep his head dry, giving him perhaps an extra hour before hypothermia set in. The ship's clerk crawled down a fender line and held onto the side of the ship, and a single passenger—the only one to survive, other than those in the lifeboats—saved himself by lying on a piece of wreckage.

The fire could be seen in Sheboygan, Wisconsin. The captains of the steamer *Delaware* and the schooner *Liberty* made ready to leave the harbor. Three hours later, the *Delaware* was the first to arrive at the scene. She approached the burned-out ship cautiously.

The captain of the *Delaware* ordered his engines to be shut down. As his ship drifted toward the *Phoenix*, the *Delaware*'s crew saw that they were too late. The *Phoenix* was burned almost to the waterline. The small amount of deck and superstructure that remained were nothing but charcoal. There was no sound from the wreck at first but, as the *Delaware* drew closer, sailors heard the faint calls of the few survivors.

Over a period of an hour, three men were pulled out of the water and five bodies were picked up from among the wreckage. The sailors on board the *Delaware* could do no more. Nearly 300 people had died in the fire or in the freezing water that surrounded it. The *Liberty* arrived at the scene in time to assist the *Delaware* in taking the wreck in tow. The *Delaware*'s captain ordered course set for Sheboygan, and his crew spent a short, sleepless night reliving the horror of the scene. One sailor later told a newspaper reporter that there wasn't a dry eye among the crew as they sailed back to Manitowoc towing the corpse of the *Phoenix*. The hulk ended up in Manitowoc harbor, where pieces of it lay for nearly a century. It's now buried under landfill from a Depression-era make-work project.

Three months after the disaster, word of the *Phoenix* tragedy reached Holland. The nation was plunged into mourning. In America, the news traveled more quickly. Relief agencies helped the few survivors to establish themselves in Wisconsin, and the descendants of Dutch survivors live in the Sheboygan and Manitowoc area today.

The story had one minor, distressing sequel. Six months after the *Phoenix* burned, a peddler appeared in Sheboygan with a cartload of charred wooden shoes, supposedly picked up along the Lake Michigan shore. They were almost certainly fakes, made through the winter and seasoned in the man's wood stove. Americans appreciate souvenirs, but this was too much. For his months of hard work, the peddler was rewarded with a quick, uncomfortable trip to the outskirts of town, and warned never to return.

Seven years after the loss of the *Phoenix*, the seventy passengers and crew aboard the steamer *E.K. Collins* found themselves in a similar dreadful situation, this time on the Detroit River. In the case of the *Collins*, however, help did arrive in time, at least for some. Fire broke out on the *Collins* as she headed downstream on the night of Sunday, October 8, 1854. The fire spread very quickly, consuming the lifeboats, and forcing the people huddled at the bow of the ship to decide whether to stick with the burning vessel or try their luck with the cold and the currents of the river.

The *Collins*, on a run from Sault Sainte-Marie to Buffalo, had just entered the main channel in the center of the river. Captain H.J. Jones of Detroit knew the river well and was piloting the vessel himself. Most of the passengers were in the ship's lounge when fire was detected in the boiler room at about 8:00 P.M. The fire killed the engine, which meant that the pumps were inoperable. The ship's big sidewheels stopped turning, leaving the *Collins* at the mercy of the river's currents. Crowds, seeing the vessel in trouble, gathered in communities along the river's edge. In Malden, now Amherstburg, Ontario, furniture seller James Bartlett was among the crowd, but left it to try to save the *Collins*'s passengers. Sailing alone in his small boat, Bartlett rescued fourteen passengers who were clinging to the *Collins*'s anchor chain, five from housing above the port wheel, and six more from the starboard wheel. He also pulled two swimmers from the water on the same trip. In all, Bartlett saved twenty-seven of the forty-four people who survived the fire on board the *Collins*. Five more were saved by the small steamer *Fintry*, skippered by a Captain Langley, which drew alongside the burning ship. Thirty-six people died that night on the Detroit River.

Ill fortune pursued the *Collins*. The burned-out steamer was converted into a barge, renamed, of all things, *The Ark*, and subsequently sank with all hands in a Lake Huron storm in 1866.

On May 21, 1867, the Northern Transportation Co. ship *Wisconsin* caught fire just after leaving Cape Vincent at the easternmost end of Lake Ontario. The *Wisconsin* was on a regular run from Ogdensburg, New York, to Chicago, with seventy passengers and twenty crewmen.

The ship left the dock at Cape Vincent at 11 P.M. Just as the ship rounded the point that separates Lake Ontario from the St. Lawrence River, a sailor ran to the bridge and told Captain Townshend there was a fire in the hold near the boiler. Townshend ordered the ship to be steered toward Grenadier Island. Sailors used pumps and hoses to try to douse the fire, but made no headway. Passengers were alerted. Townshend ordered the lifeboats to be made ready, but instructed that no one be allowed into them until he gave the order. The tragedy of the *Wisconsin* is that many people chose not to obey the captain: many men, women, and children raced for the boats.

Five members of the Chisholm family of Chateauguay, Quebec—Catherine, 42, Elizabeth 20, Mary Anne, 17, Catherine, 15, and Thomas, 11—were placed in the lifeboat by their father, Robert. At one lifeboat, crowded with twenty people, men hacked at the rope with jackknives until the bow rope broke. The people in the boat were tossed into the cold water of Lake Ontario where they quickly either drowned or died of hypothermia. Some of them may have lived long enough to see the *Wisconsin* run aground on Grenadier Island. Those who listened to the captain and stayed calm were taken off the boat by the surviving crew.

The Chisholm children were buried at Cape St. Vincent. Seventeen years later, the body of their father, who had survived the fire, was brought to the cemetery to join them.

Like the *Collins*, the *Seabird* was a sidewheel steamboat, built in 1859 in the shipyard of Eber Brock Ward in Marine City, Michigan. The *Seabird* was about 190 feet long and could carry 444 tons. Passengers were housed on two decks. The ship was fitted out with 50 cabins and enough third-class sleeping space for 200 passengers.

On April 8, 1868 the *Seabird* set out on an early-season run to Chicago from Two Rivers, Wisconsin. Fortunately, she was, at best, half full, with between fifty and 100 passengers and crew. At about 4:30 A.M., as the ship sailed about five miles from the Wisconsin shore, a porter tried to get rid of some hot coals from a cabin stove by tossing them over the ship's stern. The strong north wind blew them back onto the lower deck, where they landed on straw. Three hours later, flames began flickering from the straw. Tubs of ship's varnish were stored nearby and, once the straw ignited, the rear half of the lower deck blazed up in a fireball. All the ship's lifeboats were located in this part of the ship and consequently were destroyed in the early going. The crew and passengers panicked as the fire spread. Again, people were faced with the same awful choice, between fire and freezing water. In this case, just three people survived: one man by holding the anchor chain of the wreck until help arrived hours later: another man who was picked up floating on a piece of wreckage; and a third who paddled to shore near Evanston, Illinois, on some lumber from the wreck. The hulk of the *Seabird* finally sank a mile offshore.

In late June, 1876, Colonel George Custer and his 7th Cavalry had their grim rendezvous with Crazy Horse and Sitting Bull in the Little Bighorn valley. The news cast a pall over, but did not completely ruin, the celebrations commemorating the 100th anniversary of independence. In the Midwest, Chicago was well on its way to being rebuilt with much more modern, permanent, and safe buildings, after the fire that had virtually destroyed the city five years earlier. It was an eventful period in American history.

Five days after the Centennial celebrations, the passenger and freight ship *St. Clair*, commanded by Captain Robert Rhynus, was on her way from Duluth to Houghton, Michigan. She had just left Ontonagon, Michigan, carrying sixteen passengers, a crew of fifteen, and a full cargo of flour, feed, grain, cattle, sheep, and hogs. The ship was about ten miles from Fourteen Mile Point when a sailor sounded an alarm that there was fire in the hold. The flames quickly spread onto the hurricane deck, destroying the yawl that was the *St. Clair*'s main lifeboat. A second, smaller boat was manhandled over the side, but in the confusion, Captain Rhynus was struck and knocked into Lake Superior. There wasn't enough room for everyone on the boat, and everyone on board knew that they would have just minutes to live in the frigid waters of Lake Superior. A melee broke out as passengers vied with crew members for a space in the boat. The lifeboat subsequently rolled several times, tossing everyone into the lake. In the end, twenty-six people died. The captain, his first mate, the ship's chief engineer, its wheelsman, and just one passenger survived.

So many Great Lakes tragedies occurred on the last run of the season. Partly, of course, it's because November and early December are a time of drastic change in the weather, as Arctic air battles with the cold waters over the lakes and the warm air wafting northward from the Gulf of Mexico. Weather was a factor in one grim ship fire, the burning of the *Clarion* off Point Pelée, Ontario, on December 8, 1909.

The *Clarion* was on her last run of the season, a trip with freight and cargo that began in Chicago and was to end in Buffalo. The wooden steamer cleared the Detroit River and had just entered the open water of Lake Erie when she was hit by a full gale. This time, when fire sprang from the hold, the sailors fought back. First Engineer Alex Welch led the *Clarion*'s crew in a four-hour battle against the flames and the wind. The effort bought them time, making possible one of the most memorable rescues in Great Lakes history. Welch later described his ordeal to a reporter:

> The intense heat had driven us to about the limit of endurance when we were rescued. The fire spread so quickly that there was no time to effect a rescue. In an incredibly short time the hold was a seething mass of flames and the boat, owing to the loss of her steering, was completely out of hand. We saw Captain Bell and the forward crew launching the big metallic lifeboat and we turned to the light wooden boat on the davits aft. Her lines were coated with ice, and long before we got them clear, Captain Bell and the other members of the crew succeeded in getting away. There we were, with a roaring furnace beneath our feet and without a boat, even if one could live in such a sea.

Welch was the senior officer to survive. First mate James Thompson died early in the evening, when he was overcome by smoke in the hold. Welch and five of his men kept their nerve, worked the ship's pumps, and lived through the ordeal. Captain Thomas Bell and the thirteen sailors who panicked and took to the lifeboats were drowned.

Those who lived to tell the tale were picked up by the *Hannah*, which spotted the burning ship as she worked her way through the treacherous passage between Point Pelée and Pelée Island. Battling waves that washed over her decks, the *Hannah* made several approaches before finally pulling alongside the burning ship. By then, the lifeboats were long gone, tumbled in the waves, and dashed on the stony beach on the west side of the point. The *Clarion* drifted, burning, until it sank off Southeast Shoal.

Sadly, the age of the Great Lakes passenger ship didn't end either gently or gracefully. While aircraft and automobiles began draining away business in the 1930s and early 1940s, the end of the era can he traced to one terrible night in Toronto harbor.

The Canada Steamship Lines steamer *Noronic*, a 6,800-tonne ship built in Port Arthur in 1913, spent September 1949 catering to late-season travelers. She was the largest cruise ship on the lakes, a rather dowdy floating hotel. She had ended her regular passenger runs to Lake Superior and was put to work taking people from Cleveland and Detroit to the Thousand Islands.

The *Noronic* arrived at Pier 9 at 7:00 P.M. on the night of Friday, September 17. The day had been calm and warm. The staff of the *Noronic* was given shore leave and the captain went into the city to visit friends. Some of the passengers also went into the city, but most stayed on board, either sleeping in their cabins, or chatting in the ship's lounge. By midnight, most of those who had been to town had made their way back to the ship.

The fire started in a linen closet near the rear of the promenade deck, at about 1:00 A.M. It was probably caused by cleaners who dumped their cigarette butts into a garbage can in the closet. Gordon Churche, a Chicago jeweler out for a walk on C deck, one of five decks on the ship, saw a strange glow through the window of a cabin. He called for help. Smoke floated from around the closet door. The paint on the door itself was beginning to bubble and flake because of the heat. When a crewman touched the handle, he burned his hand.

Instead of leaving the fire alone until they were armed with a hose, one of the people standing by the closet opened the door. The fire exploded from the closet, leapt to the wooden walls and trim, and spread quickly through the cabin decks where passengers slept. Many died in their sleep.

In the days that followed, crew members offered various reasons why the alarm wasn't sounded right away. There was an alarm on the pier, but no one pulled the switch until twenty minutes after the closet door was opened. A number of observers speculated later that the fire could have been contained if the Toronto fire department had been called at an earlier stage.

When the alarm was finally set off, eighteen fire trucks and a fire-fighting boat were at Pier 9 within a matter of minutes. Next came fleets of police and ambulances. And then hearses.

Chief engineer Fred Bonnell was sleeping in his cabin when one of the crew called into the room that the ship was

on fire. Bonnell pulled on his pants and went to the fire-
alarm indicator board to see how far the blaze had spread.
By the time he reached the indicator he couldn't see it for the
smoke. The chief engineer went back to his cabin to try to
retrieve the ship's log and some other important papers, but
his way was blocked by smoke and flames.

There was panic as passengers understood the danger
they were in. People trampled one another in stairwells. In
many cases, they struggled to the top of a companionway
only to find their way blocked by fire. It was luck rather than
ship-board disaster preparations, or the skill of the Toronto
Fire Department, that would determine who survived. Able-
bodied people had a good chance to get off the *Noronic* if
they were prepared to jump about twelve feet into the relatively warm water of the harbor. Many of the passengers,
however, were older people. The tiny crew, untrained in fire
rescue, had no idea what to do. For a short time Bonnell
wandered the deck helplessly. As the fire spread toward him
in the bow, people on the dock urged him to get off the ship
and, after a minute or so of indecision, he did. He had done
nothing to save the passengers.

One witness said the *Noronic* "went up like a paint factory." It was a fitting description. The partition walls inside
her hull were dry timber; the staircase walls were made of
pine; hardwood panelling covered the walls of the ship's
lounge. The ship had neither a sprinkler system nor fire-
proof bulkheads. Nearly every year, her interior had been
spruced up with a new coat of oil-based paint. In some
places, the paint was more than thirty layers thick. And,
while the ship's hull was made of steel, most of the cabin area
was wooden.

Captain William Taylor was sixty-five and close to retirement. He arrived back at his ship just after the firefighters. Like most of the crew, Taylor had spent the evening in the city's bars. Later, he was faulted for being drunk, but by the time he arrived at Pier 9, there was nothing he could have done. He was not much more than a bystander. Later, he told a reporter of his attempts to assist passengers:

I threw water and made as much noise as possible to arouse people and one of the crew and several other people came and helped me. We broke open windows but there were no passengers in those rooms. We found a woman who had fainted and carried her to the deck below so that she could be carried out through the gangway from the engine room. The fire at this time was aft to the midships door and we did our best to put out the fire in that section. But a room would go "pfft," like that, and the windows would blow out, and the whole thing would be ablaze. I ran forward to the bow, where Mate Gerry Wood was putting people over the side with a rope. I went back and fought as long as I could on that side and then went down to D deck. The rooms of the crew and passengers were open with no one in them.

Members of the crew kept hollering for me to get out of there as the fire was coming down. I visited the crew's quarters aft and went down through the engine room and from there out to the dock. I asked people there, "Are you sure everyone is out?" and decided that they could not be. I went back to C deck and it was ablaze all the way through. It was hot there. I went a second time to D deck and used the hose again. Water was, by that time, up to the doorjamb. A stout kid was with me and we walked in water up to our knees. We had to hold our breath to keep from getting smothered and we came out on the dock again through the engine room. I went along the dock to the bow to see whether I could see anyone on board, and tried to get back, but people on the dock tried to stop me. I guess I wasn't polite to them.

For most of the rest of the night, the shattered captain was crumpled on the dock, watching the misery on board his ship. Just before dawn, he was taken to the *Kingston*, a passenger ship near the *Noronic*'s dock, and put to bed in one of its cabins.

Jacqueline Turner, a young woman who had been returning to the city from Toronto Island, saved at least six dazed and traumatized people who floated among the embers and wreckage.

One woman dropped like a stone into the water near us. I saw many people clambering down the ladders and ropes. We would pick up one victim from the bay at a time and rush them to the dock or the life-saving cruiser and go back for another. Someone warned us to get away from the fire at the stern where we were because it was getting worse.

Ross Leitch, the driver of another water taxi, helped save more than 100 people. He had seen the fire from Toronto Island, went to the fire station there, and wakened the men on duty. Then he scooted across the harbor.

When he arrived, he found mayhem. People poured over

the side of the ship in a mad scramble to survive. The first person he saved was a woman suspended halfway between the *Noronic*'s deck and the water. Leitch helped her into his boat. Then he turned to the mass of people in the boat channel. As he pulled people from the water and drove them to the dock or the life-saving boat, his boat filled up with bloody clothes. Sometimes, people in the water grabbed the side of his small boat, nearly capsizing it. With the help of two other men, he managed to haul people into the water taxi and steer it to shore, even when people were still hanging onto the sides. All the while, he could hear the terrible noise from the *Noronic*, the screams, the shouts, and the steady wail of the ship's siren.

Leo Kari, an eighteen-year-old busboy, was sleeping in his cabin near the stern when the fire broke out. The mayhem on deck woke him up. After pushing through the crowd of distraught passengers on deck, he found his way to a lifeboat. Somehow, he and several other crewmen were able to launch it. None of the *Noronic*'s other boats left the ship that night. Most either melted or burned. "We couldn't get the lifeboat free because the ropes were stuck," he told a reporter. "I remember struggling back to my cabin through the smoke. I tried to find a jackknife to cut the rope. I couldn't see a thing." When he got back to the lifeboat, none of the passengers seemed to want to get in it. Three women passengers were panicking. Karl helped to grab them and shove them into the boat. By then, most of the other passengers were gone. "We looked for other passengers but they were at the front. We could hear them shouting. But it was useless to try and go through that fire. We had to shove off with an almost empty boat or we wouldn't have got away at all."

Kari's friend, Jack Brough, an eighteen-year-old bellhop from Sarnia, used a fire ax to smash windows on the promenade deck to get to passengers who were trapped in their cabins. Some of the passengers he found were unconscious. Brough pulled a man and a woman from one cabin and rescued another woman who lay in a pool of water that had been blasted into her cabin by the firefighters.

Some passengers were in shock. They seemed to have no idea what was going on around them. Others were so weak from smoke inhalation that they had to be dragged to the *Noronic*'s deck.

Along the ship's deck and on the gangplank, many of the passengers were carrying trunks and suitcases. Not satisfied with saving themselves, they were trying to save their luggage, too. Suitcases broke open as people pushed against each other, showering clothes into the harbor and onto the pier. People trying to hold onto their luggage clogged the two gangplanks at a terrible cost to the people behind them.

Passengers wandered aimlessly through the mass of firefighters and spectators on the pier. Some were looking for lost family members. Wives and husbands often were separated and taken to different hospitals and first-aid stations, so many individuals didn't know whether their spouses were alive or dead, injured or safe. The din was frightful: people aboard the doomed ship shouted and screamed, their cries often echoed by horrified witnesses on the dock. Fire engine and ambulance sirens wailed through the night. The noise could easily be heard half a mile away. Except for the terrible sounds made by the trapped and dying passengers, the row didn't stop until morning.

In the days after the disaster, the shattered relatives of the

Noronic's dead passengers arrived in the city. Most hoped that somehow the first reports they had heard would turn out to be wrong, that somehow their kin were safe. Sometimes the dead were recognizable only by a piece of jewelry, or the specific details of remnants, like the buttons on their clothes. The first newspaper stories put the number of the dead among the ship's crew at sixty, which left little hope for their families. Those reports were wrong: all the crew were either off the ship or had been saved.

The city rallied to help the *Noronic*'s survivors with donations of clothes, cash, blood, work, anything they might need. A makeshift morgue was set up at the city's exhibition grounds. Undertakers donated their services. Several volunteer secretaries stayed up all night typing lists of survivors and of people known to have died. Members of the clergy, in their role as the era's version of today's grief counselors, consoled anyone who needed them.

In the end, the fire claimed 118 lives. Dozens more were seriously hurt.

Two days after the fire, the Canadian government ordered an inquiry. The hearing gave the passengers of the *Noronic* a chance to vent their anger at the crew and captain. The commission's report blamed the crew, but also criticized the ship's owners for not installing proper safety equipment. Captain Taylor was given a three-month suspension of his master's license by a naval tribunal. His reputation was ruined, his career at an end.

The commission's report made rather reasonable recommendations to improve safety. But the Great Lakes passenger trade was dying. Within a few years, the Interstates and the Trans-Canada highway finished it off.

Rather than incurring the expense of upgrading their ships, most of the owners of Great Lakes passenger boats sold them for scrap. By the 1960s, except for ferries and a few charter boats, passenger ships had disappeared from the lakes. From time to time, there have been attempts to revive them. In the summer of 2004, regular ferry service began between Rochester, New York, and Toronto, but by the end of that season, the plan was hobbled by lawsuits, problems with Customs, and serious doubts about the demand for the service. That service, or others like it, may yet breathe life into what seems to be an outdated way of traveling. If that happens, the ship owners can look back to the safety lessons learned the hard way in the century when the Great Lakes formed the highway to the West.

Ship fires effectively finished off the Great Lakes passenger trade. Fire is also responsible for the last major accident on the Great lakes, the burning of the full-sized lake freighter *Cartiercliffe Hall* on June 5, 1979, eleven miles off Copper Harbor, Michigan.

The 730-foot Canadian ship, under the command of Captain Raymond Boudreau, was homeward-bound on Lake Superior with a full load of corn for Port Cartier, Quebec. At 3:50 A.M., a watchman saw flames coming from the crew quarters on the port-side main deck. Very soon afterwards, the fire penetrated into the pilothouse and officer's deck. Second Mate James Hancock had only a moment to order the engine room to stop the ship. Wheelsman Jean Pruneau was able to sound the alarm just seconds before smoke and fire drove both men from their posts. There was no time to use the ship's whistle or send a mayday signal, and the general alarm system stopped working soon after Hancock and Pruneau fled the bridge.

Nineteen crewman survived, many of them by smashing windows to escape from their cabins. Four men died in their beds, while two more became confused by the smoke and staggered into the burning stern area. Captain Boudreau and three of his crew were badly burned. The first mate ordered lifeboats to be lowered and kept alongside the ship. Twenty minutes later, afraid the fire would reach the fuel tank, the captain ordered the ship to be abandoned. It was the last time in that century that a Great Lakes vessel was abandoned by her crew.

Before leaving, several sailors fired off flares, which were spotted by the crew of U.S. Steel's ore carrier *Thomas W. Lamont*. Captain William D. Wilson ordered his ship to make for the fire scene, nine miles away, at full speed. Within minutes, they were joined in their mission by four other lake freighters: the *Arthur B. Homer, Louis R. Desmarais, A.H. Ferbert,* and *Philip D. Block.* Coast guard helicopters and fixed wing aircraft were scrambled from Traverse City, Michigan, and two Canadian Coast Guard cutters, the *Bayfield* and the *Griffon,* also hurried to the scene.

By the time the *Lamont* arrived, forty-five minutes after her crew spotted the first flares, the *Cartiercliffe Hall* was burning furiously. Nineteen men were taken from the lifeboats. The four badly burned men were flown to the University of Michigan's Burn Center in Ann Arbor. Doctors could not save Third Mate Paul Boisvert, who died weeks after the fire.

The *Cartiercliffe Hall* was towed to Thunder Bay, Ontario, where city firefighters extinguished the last sparks and embers and found the bodies of the six men who died on the ship.

CHAPTER EIGHT

Alexander McDougall's Whalebacks

IN THE SUMMER OF 1890, people living along the upper Great Lakes saw a steamer that looked more like a submarine than a lake freighter. The freighter *Colgate Hoyt* was like something out of a Jules Verne novel. The typical freighter in those days had sharp lines, but this ship had been rounded off. Even the pilothouse no longer towered above the deck, but was set snugly into it. People in port cities around the lakes flocked to the docks to see it.

The *Hoyt*, though far different from the hundreds of other ships on the lakes, had an appealing look to her. The rounded hull and superstructure were somehow comforting. The shape suggested that the waves would roll harmlessly over the boat instead of pushing against flat, vertical surfaces. The *Hoyt* and her descendants, which rolled out of a

Duluth, Minnesota, shipyard in staggering numbers over the next eight years, were dubbed "whalebacks" by sailors and newspaper writers. This type of ship was a unique Great Lakes creation.

Alexander McDougall was the father of the whalebacks. He was born in Scotland in 1845. He received just two years of primary school education in Glasgow before emigrating to Canada with his family when he was eight years old. Those two years of schooling were the only formal education he would get. Whatever learning he acquired after that came by reading and observing. His classroom was the Great Lakes. When he was fifteen, he landed a job as a deckhand on the steamer *Edith*. Ten years later, he earned his master's papers and became one of the youngest captains on the lakes. He was also one of the smartest. Word of his brilliance got around to ship owners and, while still in his twenties, McDougall was offered command of some of the best vessels.

McDougall was appalled by the loss of life and the waste of ships and cargoes on the Great Lakes. Three or four ships were lost every year in the last third of the nineteenth century. Weather was by far the greatest cause of ship disasters, and boats lost to storms all too often took their entire crew with them. McDougall wanted to stop those losses and, in his spare time, began designing a hull that could handle any Great Lakes storm. He saw that most ships were unable to cope with high waves that washed over their decks and clawed at hatchways. Once a storm had the power to send waves over the hull of a loaded freighter—on some ships, just a few feet—the ship was extremely vulnerable.

McDougall's idea was simple: make the deck watertight,

let the waves roll unimpeded over the top, and rely on the buoyancy of the sealed hull to keep the ship afloat. Essentially, whalebacks rode like surfaced submarines. McDougall, however, did not borrow the idea from submarines. In fact, the reverse may be true. The first real subs—German U-boats—weren't built until a decade later. It's quite likely that German engineers borrowed ideas from McDougall's designs, which, by then, were known throughout the world.

McDougall used his own money to build the first whaleback vessel on the lakes, *Barge 101*, in 1888. While many sailors and ship owners were skeptical of the design, it captured the imagination of John D. Rockefeller, America's first billionaire. He had the money to take a good idea and make it work. The year after *Barge 101* started working the lakes, McDougall's shipbuilding company, underwritten by Rockefeller, was incorporated in Duluth. The year after that, the *Hoyt* was launched by the American Steel Barge Company. It was the first of forty-four whaleback steamers and barges that were built in the next few years. Its design was so complex that the stern and bow had to be built separately by a state-of-the-art shipyard in Wilmington, Delaware. All but one of the whalebacks were freighters.

The whalebacks were fast, averaging fifteen knots, powerful (they were designed to tow large whaleback barges), cheap to build, and inexpensive to operate. Sailors didn't like them because they required a smaller crew. The competition despised them, because the streamlined hull saved on fuel. Other shipyards denigrated the whalebacks out of fear and envy. A person could easily tell where someone stood on McDougall's ships: while supporters called them "whalebacks,"

A great many whalebacks were made in a short time in McDougall's shipyards.

opponents called them "pigboats." If the view held by vested interests along the Great Lakes had been decisive, the whalebacks would be remembered today as a folly, one man's futile attempt to change an entire industry. It's true that McDougall's ships left no more than a trace of a legacy on the lakes, but they failed for reasons that had nothing to do either with business or safety, the two reasons that should count the most.

While engineers and business leaders on the lakes remained skeptical, their counterparts abroad and along the ocean coasts of North America were far more open to McDougall's ideas. A full-sized whaleback steamer, the *Charles W. Whetmore*, crossed the Atlantic in 1891, and was closely examined by intrigued engineers from Britain and Europe. Shipyards on both sides of the Atlantic and along Europe's major inland waterways began incorporating McDougall's designs into their own. The Doxford and Sons shipyard in England began turning out whalebacks in 1893, and then created its own "Turret Ship," which used

McDougall's cigar-shaped hull, conical bow and stern design. Turret ships served as workhorses, in the English coastal trade for years. The *Whetmore* went on to sail through the Suez Canal, visited ports in Asia, and crossed the Pacific Ocean. She impressed California engineers and U.S. Navy officers before heading north to Everett, Washington. There, McDougall, still using Rockefeller money, opened his second shipyard, and began turning out whalebacks for the Pacific coast trade.

McDougall was generous with his ideas, allowing foreign engineers to examine his ships and copy his designs. He was not overly protective of his patent rights. Neither, however, was he a poor businessman. He moved his Duluth shipyard to a larger lot across the harbor and began a program of ship-building that wouldn't be matched in speed and efficiency until the Kaiser shipyards began turning out Liberty ships in World War II, some fifty years later. McDougall used a version of the assembly line to build ships years before Henry Ford incorporated the concept to make cars. In its first year of operation, McDougall's yard worked on ten ships simultaneously, and then launched one ship every Saturday for eight weeks in the summer of 1893. On the ninth Saturday, it launched two full-sized freighters and a tug.

McDougall's shipyard built nineteen whaleback freighters, one passenger vessel, and twenty-three consort barges between 1889 and 1898. The passenger ship *Christopher Columbus* was a remarkable vessel. She had two decks perched on four cylindrical turrets that were anchored into the hull of the ship. The *Christopher Columbus* was built for the 1893 World's Fair in Chicago. After her unveiling in front of a huge crowd, she was kept busy that summer carrying tens of

The extraordinary design of the passenger ship Christopher Columbus *is evident in this photograph.*

thousands of people from Great Lakes cities to Chicago's waterfront. From 1893 until she was scrapped in 1936, she was the most popular vessel on the lakes and carried more passengers in her lifetime than any other ship on the inland seas. The *Christopher Columbus* was equipped with all kinds of accoutrements and gadgetry—even including a bicycle track. Her distinctive shape and brilliant white hull made her a jewel in any port she visited. So why weren't more built? No shipping company wanted one.

The McDougall shipyard's construction statistics show that, after the initial rush, demand for the whalebacks declined. Competitors tried to undercut McDougall by designing "turtlebacks," "monitors," and "straightbacks," all of which used some of McDougall's concepts. One such ship, the "semi-whaleback" *Andaste,* was built in Cleveland in 1892. She sank on September 9, 1929 in a Lake Michigan gale, with the loss of her entire crew of twenty-five. It was the worst disaster on the lakes involving a whaleback-type vessel. The wreck has never been found.

Very few true whalebacks were wrecked. The first two disasters involving McDougall's boats were caused by the negligence of the captains of other lake boats. In 1901, the whaleback *Sagamore* was hit by the steamer *Northern Queen* near the Lake Superior entrance to the Sault Ste. Marie locks. Her crew escaped unharmed. In a much more serious accident, on June 7, 1902, the whaleback freighter *Thomas Wilson* left Duluth carrying a full cargo of Mesabi iron ore. Several of her hatches were open—her captain intended to have them closed and fastened as the ship began her run down the lake. The weather was fair, the lake was calm, and there was no reason to expect problems.

Meanwhile, the wooden steamer *George Hadley*, loaded with coal, was approaching the harbor entrance. She was scheduled to unload in Duluth but, because that city's piers were crowded, the tug *Annie L. Smith* signalled the *Hadley* to change course to Superior. Without looking, the captain of the *Hadley* ordered an immediate turn to port. The *Wilson* lay low in the water and was fairly easy to miss. The *Wilson's* captain tried to steer his heavy ship out of the way, but the *Hadley* plowed into her bow. The *Wilson* heeled over to port and, within four minutes, sank by the bow. Nine of the *Wilson's* crew went down with her. Eleven survived. The *Hadley*, which was taking water through a gash in her bow, was able to beach herself and was eventually repaired and re-floated.

The *James B. Colgate*, built in 1892, was among the last three ships built at McDougall's original Duluth shipyard.

She was one of the first full-sized whaleback freighters built to carry grain, coal, and iron ore to ports between Lake Superior and Buffalo. In 1898, while headed north in Whitefish Bay, she ran into a vicious storm. The seas were so powerful that two hull plates near the pilot house were split apart. Her captain turned the ship around and raced the leaking *Colgate* back into the Soo. Engineers there were amazed to discover that, while the steel was broken by the force of the storm, none of the rivets installed at the McDougall shipyard had failed. Her construction was literally stronger than steel.

For the next eighteen years, she was a workhorse, easily surviving the Great Storm of 1913, which had claimed the pride of the lakes fleet—but no whalebacks. When she loaded a cargo of coal at Buffalo on Friday, October 20, 1916, for her owners, the Standard Transit Company, she seemed to be embarking on a typical fall trip. Her destination was Fort William (now Thunder Bay), Ontario, a place that was then a good market for Pennsylvania hard coal. By the end of the day, she would be the first whaleback to sink because of weather.

Storms on Lake Erie are different from those on the rest of the lakes. Most of the major storms that cleared the lakes of their ships, blows like the Great Storm and the Armistice Day Storm of 1940, caused few losses on Lake Erie. When the lake does take a solid hit by a cyclone, however, very few vessels are safe in the open. The shallowness of the lake forces the long-wave energy of storm waves into a more confined space, creating huge white-capped rollers. The *Colgate*'s crew could not know that, when their boat was leaving Buffalo that day, she was

1894 Whaleback freighters carrying ore and grain in canal, Sault Ste. Marie.

headed into a storm that would take any ship that hadn't made port by the time the center of the low pressure system passed overhead. The wind was rising and waves were breaking over the Buffalo breakwater when the *Colgate* cast off her lines just after midnight, but weather was rarely a worry to the captains of whalebacks. The ship was believed to be in good shape. She had passed a government inspection just two weeks before.

She was skippered by Captain Walter Grashaw who had been promoted from first mate just a few weeks earlier. He had been in that job for a decade. Grashaw, like so many other captains of doomed ships, had seen the weather report's storm warning, but chose to disregard it.

When the *Colgate* was just off Long Point, a third of the way down Lake Erie, the winds reached hurricane strength. Water began entering the ship's hold, and by mid-afternoon the ship's pumps were overwhelmed. There was no doubt among the crew that the *Colgate* was doomed. She developed a strong list to port and began settling at the bow end. The *Colgate* had no radio, so the crew tried to attract rescuers with searchlights and blasts of the ship's whistle. At about 10:00 P.M., the bow of the Colgate slipped under the waves about eight miles southwest of Erieau, Ontario. Her crew struggled in the water, seizing upon any wreckage that could help keep them afloat. Only three of them were able to grab onto anything substantial. Captain Grashaw, the Colgate's second engineer, and a coal passer scrambled aboard a small life raft.

The waves flipped the flimsy craft several times over the course of the night and, by dawn, Grashaw was alone. The storm had passed, the waves had settled down, and he was drifting some thirty miles west of where his ship had gone down. Grashaw was soaked, bitterly cold, and, as the day wore on, hypothermia began setting in. Through the next night, he sat bolt upright in the raft, on the verge of death. The next dawn, after a day and a half drifting on the lake, the *Colgate's* captain was spotted by the crew of the car ferry *Marquette & Bessemer No. 2*. He was hoisted aboard on a makeshift stretcher and taken to the

Marquette and Bessemer No. 2's boiler room to warm up and revive.

In the days after the *Colgate* sank, her owners tried to make sure that the lake, not the company, was blamed for the loss. Company manager H.M. Dinham, who spoke to newspaper reporters on behalf of Standard Transit, reminded them of the recent inspection: "There is no reason to believe that since then she had weakened so that she would spring a leak as the dispatches credited to Capt. Grashaw said. I am sure that he was misquoted or misunderstood." Dinham went on to say that the Grashaw's predecessor as captain, "told me today that the *Colgate* was a staunch boat and he does not believe in the leak theory. She must have been overwhelmed by the weight of the seas."

More than fifty sailors died on Lake Erie on Black Friday. The schooner *D.L. Filer* went down and only the captain, who clung to the mast, was rescued. Four others drowned. The Canadian steamer *Merida*, with twenty-three on board, was lost with all hands. She was sighted once on Black Friday in the west end of the lake by Captain Massey of the steamer *Briton*. The men on board the *Briton* knew the *Merida* was lost, but could do nothing to help. They barely made it to shelter in the lee of Point Pelée. Captain J.W. Parsons of the *Calcite* also spotted the *Merida* off the Southeast Shoal, realized she was in trouble, but believed she would make it through the storm.

"The seas at the time were about the worst I ever encountered," Captain Parsons told a newspaper reporter a few days later. "I was going head into and shipping big ones over her bow. Nearly all our dishes were broken and the furniture was badly smashed. The *Merida* was making very bad weather of it, but she kept plugging ahead. We were kept busy watching our own boat, but the *Merida* did not make any appeal for aid. Captain Jones evidently believed he would make Long Point alright."

The lumber carrier *Marshall F. Butters*, loaded with shingles for Cleveland, carried a crew of thirteen. When the ship developed a list, Captain McClure ordered the crew to toss the deck cargo overboard, but it was too late. He sounded the ship's whistle in a last attempt to get help. Two full-sized freighters, the *Frank R. Billings* and the *F.G. Hartwell*, challenged the twenty-foot waves and the seventy-mile-an-hour wind to pick up three men from a lifeboat. The captain and ten sailors who had stayed on the *Butters* were rescued with a lifeline. It was a dramatic and brave act of seamanship, made all the more poignant when, just as the last of the crew was taken off, the *Butters* slipped under the waves.

For almost seventy-five years, the location of the *Colgate's* wreck remained a mystery, one that challenged and frustrated scores of divers and shipwreck hunters. In 1991, she was located by Wheatley, Ontario, commercial fisherman Len Cabral, who spotted it with side-scan sonar when he moved his boat to Erieau. She lies upside-down in eighty-five feet of water. Much of her plating is gone. The rudder and four-bladed propeller are highlights of the wreck.

Few other whalebacks had as dramatic an end. Most, like the passenger ship *Christopher Columbus*, ended their days ingloriously in a scrap yard. The only whaleback wreck in Lake Michigan, the tanker *Henry Cort*, lies off Muskegon, Michigan. The *Cort* was tossed onto the Muskegon breakwater on November 30, 1934, after losing a fight with one of the worst storms recorded on Lake Michigan. The Coast

Guard cutter *Escanaba* braved the storm to attempt a rescue. Several of the cutter's crewmen, using the cutter's twenty-six-foot whaleboat, clawed their way through the heavy waves and strong back current and saved all twenty-five members of the Cort's crew. The rescue was marred by the loss of one of their own. John Diepert, a Coast Guardsman, was swept from the lifeboat and drowned in the surf off the ice-covered breakwater.

Whalebacks had become something of a curiosity by this time. The last whaleback, aptly named the *Alexander McDougall*, was built in 1898. Over the course of the decade in which whalebacks were built, the ships underwent many design changes. The *McDougall* was a transitional type with a conventional bow mounted on a whaleback hull. The whalebacks became obsolete when it became apparent that their design could not be adapted to new developments in cargo-handling machinery. By World War II almost all of the whalebacks had been scrapped.

The only surviving whaleback above water is the SS *Meteor*, formerly the *Frank Rockefeller*. She was renamed after being converted from a freighter to an oil tanker in 1943. The *Meteor* was taken out of service in 1969 after sustaining hull damage by running aground. She survives because of the hard work of historically minded citizens in Superior, Wisconsin. They convinced the city to buy the *Meteor* and use her as the main attraction of a museum on Barker's Island in the city's harbor.

McDougall lived to see the decline of the Great Lakes whalebacks. Whatever disappointment he may have felt was tempered by the knowledge that his ships had found homes in the ports of the English Channel and on the great rivers of Europe. By the time he died in 1924 McDougall, a very wealthy man, owned hundreds of patents, including one for refining taconite to iron ore. He developed seven shipyards that built and operated 200 ships, founded the Highland Power Company (later Minnesota Power and Allete), and organized Duluth's Northern City Bank (now part of the Wells-Fargo system). He lobbied for the St. Lawrence Seaway. And he had one last dream that has not yet come true: he looked forward to the creation of a new state, "Superior," that would incorporate the upper peninsula of Michigan, northeastern Wisconsin, and the Canadian Shield country of Minnesota. There's still time.

CHAPTER NINE

Four Mysteries

RENÉ ROBERT CAVALIER DE LA SALLE was a man whose vision and ability were not matched by his luck. He was a gambler, a man who took chances that bordered on recklessness. He lived one step ahead of his many, many creditors. He deliberately set out to steal the fur trade from the merchants of Montreal. Then he tried to do the same thing to the battle-hardened Iroquois along Lake Ontario. It's a wonder he survived in Canada as long as he did. But it was a Frenchman, not an Iroquois, who put a bullet in his back. And that happened in a lonely corner of Texas, not in the Great Lakes country.

La Salle tried leapfrogging the French and Irooquis by building forts at Kingston, Ontario, and Niagara. Then he went to work building ships. He reckoned that an armed brigantine would put the canoe-bound Iroquois out of the fur business. At the same time, he would sail past rival

French traders and the Jesuit priests who hated him. He would sail beyond them to another world. The discovery of the Mississippi had changed his whole vision. He was convinced that there were huge new lands to exploit in the west that would feed into his Great Lakes operations.

The new ship wouldn't be the first sailing vessel on the Great Lakes. In the 1640s, Jesuit priests at their mission on southern Georgian Bay had traveled the inland sea in their shallop, and La Salle himself had built boats on Lake Ontario. But the vessel he had in mind would be the first full-sized ship on the lakes above Niagara, a vessel capable of long voyages, far from land, and in hostile waters. There would be five cannon on board. The Iroquois and LaSalle's French rivals had none.

La Salle and a group of hired men began building the ship at a creek mouth near the site of what is now Buffalo, New York, in the winter of 1675. She was the *Griffin*. She was about sixty feet long, the size of a large sailing yacht. On board, at least on the up-bound voyage was a fairly skilled crew, two Recollet friars, and La Salle himself.

All they needed was a chart. Not only did La Salle lack nautical charts of the lakes themselves, but the maps of the shoreline that had been drawn by earlier explorers were wrong. For example, two generations of French cartographers had drawn a large bay on the Lake Huron side of the base of the Bruce Peninsula. What is really there is a dangerous, unprotected shoreline of rocks and sandbars. A ship whose captain depended on these maps and who got into trouble along Manitoulin Island or the Bruce Peninsula would have made for this bay—and been wrecked. If an explorer, a trader, or a native told a map maker about some island or bay that he thought he had seen, the artist drew it into his map, and subsequent cartographers copied the error. The Lake Huron ghost harbor didn't disappear from maps until the end of the 1700s.

Before La Salle, no one had tried to map the shoals farther out in the lakes simply because they had no ships for the task. They could get advice from natives, but few of the aboriginal people had been out of sight of land in their small craft.

The only eyewitness to write a description of the *Griffin's* voyage to the lakes was an unreliable character, a Recollet friar named Louis Hennepin. The European discovery of Niagara Falls has been credited to Hennepin, probably because Étienne Brulé, who saw it first, was killed and eaten by the Huron before he could put the discovery in writing. Hennepin wrote a description of the falls that has never been surpassed, mostly because it's not true: readers back in Europe, where his books were bestsellers, learned that the falls were eight miles wide and 600 feet high.

On August 7, the *Griffin's* crew and passengers finally began their trip. In all, Hennepin wrote, there were thirty-four men, including himself and another Recollet friar. The *Griffin* sailed west-southwest and traveled sixty miles the first night. The next day she sailed past Long Point and Point Pelée, clearing the hazardous strait between the southern tip of mainland Canada and Pelée Island. Later, he was terrifically impressed by the broad Detroit River and the fertile meadow that embraced it. Given the chance, Hennepin would have founded a city there, as evidenced by his report:

The forests are chiefly made up of walnut trees, chestnut trees, plum trees and pear trees, loaded with their own fruit and vines. There is also an abundance of timber fit for building, so that those who shall be so happy as to inhabit that noble country, cannot but remember with gratitude those who have discovered the way, by venturing to sail upon an unknown lake for above one hundred leagues. That charming strait lies between 40 and 41 degrees northern latitude....

I endeavored also to persuade him [LaSalle] to make a settlement upon this charming strait.... M. La Salle would by no means harken to my advice, and wondered at my proposal, considering the great passion I had a few months before for the discovery of a new country.

The *Griffin* sailed across Lake St. Clair. With some hauling by its crew and careful depth soundings, it made its way up the St. Clair River to the upper lakes. So far, the worst that had happened was a few groundings on sand bars. When they reached Lake Huron, the men aboard the *Griffin* began their education in the power of the Great Lakes. The French—their traders, explorers, and missionaries had been canoeing the edges of the lake for almost seventy years. The part they were most familiar with, however, was Georgian Bay, not the open lake to the west. The *Griffin* sailed just off the Michigan shore, nearly running aground on rocks several times. A storm that began on August 26 intensified just after the *Griffin* passed the mouth of Saginaw Bay. The crew took down the ship's mainsail and let her run at the mercy of the wind.

Hennepin wrote that most of the crew and passengers

were ready to make their peace with God. There was just one exception, the seven-foot-tall pilot, Luc: "Therefore, everybody fell upon his knees to say his prayers, and prepared himself for death, except our pilot (Luc the Dane), whom we could never oblige to pray, and he did nothing at all except to curse and swear against La Salle, who, as he said, had brought him thither to make him perish in a nasty lake, and lose the glory that he had acquired by his long and happy navigations on the Ocean." But instead of going to Heaven, they went to Mackinaw.

The Huron and Ottawa who lived at Michilimackinac, the old fort at Mackinaw, were allies of the French and enemies of the Iroquois. But the Huron and the Ottawa made their living carrying furs to Montreal. The *Griffin* threatened to put all of them out of work.

La Salle, dressed in a scarlet cloak decorated with gold lace, accompanied by sailors carrying guns, visited the leaders of the natives while some Ottawas came aboard the *Griffin* carrying gifts of whitefish and trout. But, as the *Griffin*'s purpose became clear, the mood in Michilimackinac turned ugly. La Salle and his crew went back aboard the *Griffin* and sailed on into Lake Michigan for about 125 miles, to a camp of Pottawattamies.

For days, the French traded and watched native dancers. While he was with the Pottawattamies, La Salle filled the *Griffin*'s hold with furs. Her captain and four crewmen were told to take her back to Niagara. LaSalle and the rest of his entourage would stay on Lake Michigan and prepare for an expedition to the Mississippi. On September 18, the *Griffin* hoisted sail and fired a salute from her cannon. That was the last the French saw of her.

Hennepin offered a commonsense explanation of what happened next:

> The ship came to an anchor to the north of the Lake of the Illinois [Michigan] where she was seen by some Savages, who told us that they advised our men to sail along the Coast, and not toward the middle of the Lake, because of the sands that make navigation dangerous when there is any high wind. Our pilot (a seven-foot hooligan named Luc the Dane), as I have said before, was dissatisfied, and would steer as he pleased, without harkening to the advice of the Savages, who, generally speaking, have more sense than the Europeans think at first. But the ship was hardly a league (three miles) from the coast, when it was tossed up by a violent storm in such a manner that our men were never heard of since, and it is supposed that the ship struck upon a sand and was there buried.

LaSalle didn't believe it. He could not find the wreck, and no one else has proved that the wooden hulks offered up as the *Griffin*'s wreck are authentic. So the *Griffin*'s fate is a mystery.

Some historians believe LaSalle's crew turned on their employer. If they did, they were never seen again. Blonde seven-foot men were noticed in seventeenth-century North America. A few others think the *Griffin* was attacked by natives, pillaged, and scuttled. But if the natives of the upper lakes, allies of the French, committed the crime, they were obliged to get rid of a large cargo of furs and to hide, forever, anything of value stolen from La Salle's ship. And they were burdened with keeping the attack secret from their families and their trading partners. Gossip traveled quickly in those days. The Iroquois' innocence is proven for the opposite reason: if they took the *Griffin*, why wouldn't they have bathed in the glory?

Probably the *Griffin* sank near where Lake Michigan and Lake Huron join. Many hulks have been offered up as La Salle's ship. Two wrecks, one near Tobermory, and the other on Manitoulin Island's northern tip, are said to be the most promising. The tales surrounding the Manitoulin wreck would seem to clinch it: the skeletons of six men dressed in French clothes were found in a Manitoulin Island cave, along with French coins and brass buttons. One of the skeletons was huge. These coins, skulls, and buttons, however, are all supposed to be lost. No one seems to know the whereabouts of the cave. There isn't much left of the ship.

The Tobermory wreck is even less complete than the one at Manitoulin. It may be the *Griffin*, but it could also be an old schooner or fishing boat. The Great Lakes are dotted with the hulks of boats that were allowed to sink or were forgotten.

So let's look at the clues we have. They are the ones presented to La Salle after they were fished out of Lake Huron or Lake Michigan: a hatch cover, some pants, a bundle of furs. They sound like the sort of debris that is often cast up after shipwrecks. The natives said they were found in the northern part of Lake Michigan. The prevailing wind, especially in fall storms, comes from the northwest. All things being normal, if they turned up downwind of the *Griffin*'s sinking, she went down somewhere between the end of Green Bay and the junction of Michigan and Huron.

That would mean the old priest, that master of creative writing, was right when he said the *Griffin* was lost just as she slipped out of sight of the main native settlements at the lake junction. Her little crew never had a chance to get lucky twice on the lakes. Up-bound, they had barely made it. Down-bound, they hardly got out of port before their journey ended.

The *Atlantic* took 250 people with her when she sank in Lake Erie off Long Point, Ontario, in the summer of 1852. She arrived at the bottom of the lake upright and relatively undamaged except for the hole in her hull. The prize for salvagers was a strongbox, really a small safe, in the purser's cabin. It carried some $36,700 in cash, a small fortune in those days.

That summer, there were a mysterious series of "firsts." The first submarine on Lake Erie made her first dive to the wreck. It was the first (and for more than a century the last) attempt to use a submersible to survey and salvage a wreck on the Great lakes. And it was the first, and only, time a submarine was accidentally lost in the open waters of the Great Lakes. The submarine's mission was secret. No one has found the sub, even though it should be in plain sight at the *Atlantic* wreck. Yet, if contemporary accounts are true, it must be there.

Lodner Phillips was a cobbler—a shoemaker—in Indiana, but he had a second line of work, one that he hoped would make him rich. He was an inventor, and his designs for a practical submarine were far ahead of his time.

Others, including steamboat designer Robert Fulton, were in the hunt for the patent for an effective U-boat. The *Turtle*, an ill-fated little submarine, had spooked the British fleet at New York during the Revolutionary War, but the technology needed work. The little submarine was propelled, very slowly, by a hand-crank. The mine that she spiked into the hull of a British warship would not disengage from the *Turtle*, and her mission turned into an involuntary kamikaze trip. The navy (and other countries' navies) thought submarines took the glamour out of marine warfare. A few progressive admirals believed the submarine might work if someone designed a boat that was relatively fast, safe, and capable of delivering a ship-killing bomb, but they would not put government money into research.

Shoemaking is the kind of work that gives a man time to think. Phillips came up with two design innovations that, in hindsight, seem fairly obvious. The original submarines were spherical or barrel-shaped. Lodner developed the cigar-shaped boat. Every successful submarine since the 1840s adopted a variation of Lodner's hull design. He also used a screw propeller for mobility. This screw was still turned by hand, but the Lodner subs were capable of a respectable four knots—a fast walking speed—and could dive to more than 100 feet. A boat like this could attack blockaders, like the British fleets that haunted the U.S. seaboard during the Revolutionary War and the War of 1812, and could be turned loose in harbors and rivers to attack enemy fleets as they landed troops.

Lodner tried to sell one to the navy but, in a decision that set it back a generation, the navy told Lodner: "No authority is known to this Bureau to purchase a submarine boat . . . the

The tragedy of the sinking of the Marquette & Bessemer No. 2 *was made worse by the murder that preceded it.*

boats used by the Navy go on not under the water." During the Civil War, he tried again, but was turned down. Instead, the Confederacy developed the first practical naval submarine, one similar to Lodner's fifteen-year-old prototypes.

Lodner built four subs. Two are known to survive. One (Lodner's second) was salvaged in the Chicago River in 1915, its discovery probably the only good thing to come from the *Eastland* disaster. Another (Lodner's third) lies on or near the *Atlantic.*

Lodner decided to try to salvage the *Atlantic*'s treasure in 1852. Details of his mission are sketchy, but the mission certainly happened. The strongbox was not recovered and the submarine was lost at the wreck site. Lodner came home empty-handed, but the submarine—if it is, in fact, still there—may have become the real treasure of the *Atlantic.*

Several Civil War era submarines have been raised recently. They've been given a lot of press, their crews have received heroes' funerals, and the boats themselves have become national treasures. Will the Lodner sub ever rise from the mud of Lake Erie? It's doubtful, unless governments in Canada are willing to spend the money to bring it to the surface. The courts have ruled the *Atlantic* belongs to Canada. So, too, does Lodner's sub. If it's still there.

It's amazing that a ship as large as the *Marquette & Bessemer No. 2* still hasn't been found. But everything about the wreck of the *Marquette & Bessemer No. 2* is a mystery. Dreadful evidence points to a hell night on Lake Erie: mutiny, murder, and a miserable death for both the guilty and the innocent on board. The *Marquette & Bessemer* was one of the least glamorous ships on the lakes, a workhorse that made her living carry railway cars of coal across the lake to feed the furnaces of homes in southern Ontario. There was irony and some justice in the fate of her murderous crew, who were found frozen, upright, encased in ice in a stolen lifeboat.

John and Robert McLeod were members of a family of Great Lakes sailors from Kincardine, Ontario. Both were qualified captains, but John, the eldest, decided to work as his brother Robert's first mate on the *Marquette & Bessemer No. 2* car ferry in the winter of 1909. He had just been married and wanted to organize his new home in Cortright, Ontario.

Most of the rest of the crew were Americans living in the *Marquette & Bessemer No. 2*'s home port, Conneaut, Ohio. The chief engineer, Eugene Wood, came from a Canadian sailing family that was just recovering from the loss of

Eugene's brother, George. He had been captain of the *Bannockburn* when she disappeared on Lake Superior in 1902. The *Bannockburn* had been in clear sight of other ships when a snow squall enveloped her for a few minutes. Then she was gone.

Another Canadian, William Wilson, from Lindsay, Ontario, was the wheelsman. Formerly a jeweler, he was considered to be one of the better crewmen in the car ferry service.

Three men worked in the galley. George R. Smith, a tall, tough, middle-aged man from Conneaut, was the steward, head of the kitchen staff. Harry Thomas, a young man from Port Stanley, was second cook. Manuel Souars, only twenty years old, was just beginning to work his way through the ranks. In all, there were thirty-three crew members. Most of these men had years of service to their credit. McLeod had been able personally to hire the people he wanted for his crew. There had never been a sign of trouble among them.

The same thing could not be said for the ship. She was only four years old, but there were ample signs that she was a death trap. The *Marquette & Bessemer No. 2* couldn't handle the work demanded of her. Her fatal error was the poor design of her rear door, which allowed water into her hold if the waves came at her from behind. In addition, dynamite had often been used to free the ship from ice jams, weakening the steel in her hull.

Captain McLeod knew of the ship's problems. He had sailed her into the waves in rough weather to try to get water from piling over the stern and filling her hold. The captain had told friends that he wanted off the *Marquette & Bessemer No. 2*. While he hadn't acted on his premonition, some of his crewmen had. By the time the ship made her last trip, it had become difficult for Captain McLeod to find good sailors who were willing to work on her. Captain McLeod had tried to get the ship's owners to spend the money to fix her problems, complaining the ship was dangerous, but they refused. Later, they would show the same stinginess when the families of her dead crew members were given only one month's pay to help them cope with the loss of their breadwinners.

December 1909 had been a bad month for weather, but the *Marquette & Bessemer No. 2* followed her normal routine. Coal cars were loaded below deck by freight yard engines in Conneaut. On Tuesday, December 7, 1909, she was filled with twenty-six carloads of coal, a carload of iron castings, and three railway flatcars of steel. A passenger, Albert Weiss, also came aboard, carrying $50,000 in cash in a briefcase. He planned to use it to buy a Canadian fish company.

The ship set out onto Lake Erie at 10:00 A.M., two hours late, with a southwest wind behind her.

What happened from that time on is partly a matter of speculation, but there is enough physical evidence to show that this was not to be an ordinary trip. There was the dangerous storm that appears in most Great Lakes shipwreck stories, but there were also other forces at work. By the time the *Marquette & Bessemer No. 2* was scheduled to reach Port Stanley, Lake Erie was being raked with seventy-mile-an-hour winds from the north. They hammered the ports on the U.S. side of the lake, tearing up houses on the shore and flooding towns.

At noon, four Conneaut fishermen saw the *Marquette &*

Bessemer No. 2 a few miles from the Ohio shore. Captain McLeod had come on deck wearing a fur coat, hollering through his megaphone. The men in the fishing boat couldn't make out what he was saying through the roar of the wind. After a while, the frustrated captain went back into the wheelhouse and the fishermen headed for home.

Throughout the night, the long-overdue car ferry battled the storm, searching for a safe port. It is quite likely that she crossed Lake Erie at least three times. People in several towns along the Ohio and Ontario shores said they heard the ship's whistle in the night. It called out through the blinding snow, hoping for a return blast from a harbor, as the car ferry tried to find the entrance to ports along both sides of Lake Erie. The captain seemed to be sailing toward any place that offered shelter, trying at the same time to keep the waves from rolling over the *Marquette & Bessemer No. 2's* poorly designed rear door. Each person who later claimed to have heard the ship said they could make out four wailing blasts of her whistle.

Even worse, something horrible was happening on board the ship. The evidence points toward mutiny and murder. A decent prosecutor would have no trouble piecing together the story of the ship's last hours and selling this version to a jury. The physical evidence found after the *Marquette & Bessemer No. 2's* sinking, along with what was known of the men involved, yield these details:

As the *Marquette & Bessemer No. 2* fought the Lake Erie storm, she began taking water over her stern car entrance. She probably listed to one side, which made it impossible to launch all four of her lifeboats. Ten members of the crew mutinied, led by Smith, the steward. The followers were galley workers Harry Thomas and Manuel Souars, along with six junior members of the crew, mostly men who worked below decks, and had seen the water pouring into the back of the ship. The identity of the tenth man is a mystery, but there is physical evidence that he existed.

Somewhere out in Lake Erie, after the cautious captain had turned his ship away from at least three ports, Smith had decided he was getting off the ship one way or another. He began working the crew, first among the galley staff, then among those below deck, to get support for a confrontation with the captain. Smith had access to all of the crew because they came into his galley for meals.

Any crew member with experience on the lakes knew that this was no ordinary storm. They wanted to be on land, even if the ship had to be run aground in the blizzard. Smith was able to sit with them while they griped, and then suggest that he could help them escape from the sinking, which was obviously going to happen.

Captain McLeod did not cooperate with the mutineers when they finally went to the bridge or assembled on a deck near one of the lifeboats. Confronted by Smith, who wielded a knife and a meat cleaver, the captain refused either to take his ship into port without knowing where the harbor entrances were, or to run it up on shore. He had given up on the idea of finding some place where a ship would answer the *Marquette & Bessemer No. 2*'s whistle. Now he was making a run for the east end of the lake, where he might find shelter in Buffalo. It was impossible to reason with the panic-stricken mutineers. There was no easy way of getting the ship to a landfall without risking her being torn apart by the waves. Abandoning her was just as suicidal, since the lifeboats would be pummeled by the storm. His logic failed to convince the mutineers. They silenced Robert McLeod by killing him.

The forensic evidence, sparse as it is, points to Smith as the man who stabbed Captain McLeod. He was one of the largest of the mutineers and the most senior in rank. Also, the murder weapons were his. There are no clues as to whether the bridge crew, including the captain's brother, tried to help the captain. The bodies of most of the officers were never found, so we'll never know if there was just one murder victim that night. There is also no sign to show whether the other twenty-two men on board the *Marquette & Bessemer No. 2* struggled to get into the usable lifeboats and were beaten back by the mutineers.

Soon after the captain's murder, the ten mutineers stopped the engines of the ship, and took to one of its green lifeboats. The men who stayed behind watched as the boat was winched toward the whitecaps and disappeared into the black night. Whether the remaining crew members re-engaged the *Marquette and Bessemer No. 2*'s engines and kept trying for a safe port, or just waited on the ship for the end, won't be known until the ship is found. She probably went down somewhere near Long Point. Divers have searched for her, spurred by the money in the purser's safe, but the only clues to her resting place have been puzzling sonar traces and some wreckage that came ashore.

The morning after the *Marquette and Bessemer No. 2* sank—it was a Wednesday—the sun came up on a green lifeboat with ten freezing, soaked men aboard. Not one of the men had thought to wear warm clothes. Nor had they even gathered up the lifeboat's oars before they launched it.

Maybe they were honest, or just in too much of a hurry, but no one robbed Weiss of his $50,000.

The cold winds piled water over the sides of the lifeboat, caking the little vessel with ice. Splashing water covered the hair of the men and began congealing on their clothes. Smith finally set aside his knife and cleaver, jamming them into the gunwales of the lifeboat. He sat upright, the blood on his apron mixing with the water of Lake Erie. Around him, the other mutineers huddled for warmth, groaning, complaining, crying, and, perhaps, praying, as exposure and frostbite drained their life away. We'll never know who the tenth mutineer was, because he decided that life wasn't worth the horror of that boat ride. He took off his clothes, folded them, carefully laid them over the stern of the lifeboat, and then jumped into Lake Erie. He had no chance of survival.

In the lifeboat, the men began to die. There was no room for the bodies to fall so most of them remained upright as each man slipped away. Only Manuel Souars, the young porter, had found any kind of shelter. He hid under a seat, beneath four bodies. Eventually, despite the fading warmth of his comrades, Souars closed his eyes and was gone, too. The lifeboat's single oar still dangled uselessly in the water, clasped by the frozen fingers of a dead crewman.

For five days, the little green boat floated on Lake Erie. Smith, the lead mutineer, sat frozen upright, as if scanning for the land that they had longed for so ardently on the *Marquette & Bessemer No. 2*'s last trip. Finally, a Pennsylvania state fishery inspection boat, the *Commodore Perry*, spotted the death boat. Instead of taking the dead men on board their tug, the *Commodore Perry*'s horrified crew tied a line to the boat, and towed it to Erie, Pennsylvania. The tug's flag was lowered to half-mast.

People already knew the *Marquette & Bessemer No. 2* was lost. A ship had seen one of her lifeboats floating empty near the middle of the lake. Whether it had held other crewmen is a mystery. Lumber from her pilothouse was picked up along the U.S. shore and some large pieces of wreckage washed up on the beach near Port Burwell, Ontario. The number four lifeboat with her frozen sailors and kitchen workers was the first proof that the crew was dead. No one, at first, suspected what had gone on in the ship's wheelhouse and boat deck on the night of the storm. People supposed, generously, that Smith had a strong but not completely unnatural affection for the knife and meat cleaver found in the lifeboat. Good carving knives, after all, are not easy to find.

In Conneaut, people went through the sad formalities of identifying the crewmen, contacting families, and holding an inquest. The bodies in the boat were thawed and laid out naked in the town morgue where they were photographed for the record. Flags in the Lake Erie town were lowered to half-mast and the local undertaker made arrangements to send the bodies home. The finding of the lifeboat was proof enough that the ship was gone. Funerals were held for all the men on the car ferry. In Conneaut, hundreds of people crowded into the auditorium of a new high school to mourn all the Ohio crew members, while in Port Stanley, separate funerals were held in the churches for the crewmen from that town.

The last evidence of that terrible night on the lake was to surface nearly a year later. Many people wished it hadn't. During the winter and early spring, the ship's other two lifeboats were found. One was in small fragments, with only its flotation tanks recognizable. The other was in two pieces, crushed on a rock near Buffalo. By the next summer, the bodies of four of the *Marquette & Bessemer No. 2*'s crewmen turned up. One of the dead men was mate John McLeod, whose body was found frozen in an ice floe just above Niagara Falls in April, 1910.

The captain waited until the fall to give his silent testimony of the terror of the 1909 storm. On October 6, 1910, the *Marquette & Bessemer No. 2*'s replacement ship, boldly bearing the same name, made her first run across Lake Erie. That same day, Captain Robert McLeod was found on Long Point.

The captain was in terrible shape. Deep slashes cut across his body. Those who found him realized that the meat cleaver and knife embedded in the gunwales of Lifeboat number four were not the innocent tools of a ship's cook. They were murder weapons. Captain McLeod's body, lying on a Lake Erie beach, bore irrefutable witness to the way they had been used on the night the *Marquette & Bessemer No. 2* went down. No one was convicted of the crime, of course. The lake had meted out her own crude justice.

In the summer of 1918, after four years of trench warfare that turned Belgium and northern France into a killing field, the Allied armies were moving forward. Headlines, most of their premature, announced that the Kaiser was soon to be brought to justice and the world would be made safe from "the Hun."

Modern technology had created weapons that favored well-entrenched defenders: the machine gun, long-range artillery, poison gas, barbed wire. Casualty lists grew until the very last day of the war, in the cold fall of 1918. Only tanks and airplanes could shift the advantage in warfare to the attacker, and that change in the arts of killing would come twenty-one years later, when the Nazi panzer divisions rolled over Poland.

On the Great Lakes, peacetime attitudes were already settling in by the summer of 1918. Workers who had lived with wartime austerity were demanding more money to cope with rampant inflation. At the Canadian Lakehead cities of Port Arthur and Fort William, workers at the city's grain elevators and port went on strike. Police brawled with strikers in the streets of Fort William. The walkouts were just a taste of the labor troubles that were to come in the next three years as North America entered a period of union radicalism, recession, and post-war industrial decline that rocked society to its foundations and spread a fear of "Reds" among politicians and the citizenry.

But in November, 1918, workers still put in long days at weapons factories. It takes months to gear a country up for total war, and almost as long to wind it down.

All these munitions plants operated as though the streets were filled with lurking Prussian saboteurs. The secrecy that cloaked Canada's war effort was backed by the toughest censorship in North American history (before or since). Armed guards patrolled bridges and railway trestles in Canada and the Unites States, looking for enemy spies. People with German names were hounded, no matter where they were born or for how many generations their families had lived in the country.

This official secrecy shrouded the construction in 1918 of a small fleet of minesweepers in Fort William, Ontario. The ships, intended for the French navy, were built at the Canada Car and Foundry Company's Fort William shipyard near the mouth of the Kamanistikwia River. They were Navarin-type minesweepers, about 140 feet long, eighty wide, and divided into four watertight compartments. Each was armed with four-inch guns in the bow and stern (in violation of the Rush-Bagot Agreement between Canada and the U.S., which prohibited more than one armed ship on each side of the Lakes). The ships looked like a cross between a navy patrol boat and a fishing trawler, with a single funnel and masts fore and aft. The minesweepers were manned by a crew of thirty-six.

The minesweepers' crews, members of the French navy, arrived in the Lakehead in the fall. The new minesweepers were named the *Inkerman*, *Cerisoles*, and *Sebastopol*, after battles in the Crimean War. There was no fanfare at their christening. After the launch, the ships had short trial runs on Lake Superior, on the far side of the Lakehead harbor's protective peninsula and islands. The minesweepers seemed to perform up to the standards set in their construction contracts, developing speeds of about twelve knots, and were said to handle well in rough water.

When the ships left Fort William on Saturday, November 3, each one had a Canadian lake pilot to help them navigate Lake Superior. The pilots on the *Inkerman* and *Cerisoles*, Captain Murphy and Captain Wilson, were seasoned Great Lakes skippers. The minesweepers steamed out of the harbor together, the *Inkerman* under the command of Captain Mezou, the *Sebastopol* skippered by Captain Leclerc, and the

Cerisoles with Captain Deude at the helm. Captain Leclerc was the overall commander of the small fleet. Before the ships left port, a member of the four-man French commission that had supervised the construction handed each of the captains an envelope of sealed orders which were to be read once the ships were out of the harbor. Henri Jacobs, the wireless operator on the *Inkerman*, had ensured the three ships could communicate with each other but no one else on the Great Lakes could receive their signals.

Midway across the lake, a day's sailing from Fort William, the fleet fought its way through a blizzard that blew from the southwest. The minesweepers, on unfamiliar waters, had no way of taking their bearings. The *Sebastopol*, sailing ahead, emerged from the blizzard on the American side of the border. She barely made it. Marius Mallor, a French sailor on the *Sebastopol*, later wrote from Port Stanley, on Lake Huron:

> Here I am after leaving Port Arthur but you can believe me that I would have preferred to have remained there because on the first night of our voyage, our boat nearly sank, and we had to get out the life boats and put on life belts—but that is all in a sailor's life. Three minutes afterwards the boat almost sank—and it was nearly "goodbye" to anyone hearing from us again.... You can believe me, I will always remember that day. I can tell you that I had already given myself up to God.

The *Sebastopol* struggled through the gale for two more days before finally reaching Sault Ste. Marie. Captain Leclerc later said he took the *Sebastopol* into the Soo locks, believing the other two ships would arrive in a few hours and join him in the St. Mary's River. On Sunday, December 1, Lieutenant Garreau, the French officer in charge of overseeing the construction of the three ships, received a telegram from Captain Leclerc, saying the *Sebastopol* had arrived in Port Colborne, at the Lake Erie end of the Welland Canal. There was nothing in the message about the *Inkerman* and the *Cerisoles*. The first public news of the possible loss of the ships arrived in Fort William on December 3, ten days after the two ships had left the city bound for Sault Ste. Marie. Still, city officials, including Fort William mayor Hy Murphy, hinted that the two ships may still be sailing somewhere on the Great Lakes, under a shroud of censorship and official secrecy.

In the next few days, rumors swept Fort William that the ships could have secretly locked through at Sault Ste. Marie without being registered because they were naval vessels. Still, tugs braved a new round of blizzards to search the islands and shoreline of northern Lake Superior. By the middle of December, after no one from the two minesweepers turned up, hope faded. People began looking for someone to blame. At first, the builders were targets, but blame eventually settled on the lake itself, and a mysterious landform that was kept secret from most Great Lakes sailors.

The seventy-eight French sailors and two Canadian skippers who went down with the French minesweepers represent the largest unexplained loss of life on the Great Lakes. Officially, no bodies ever came ashore. A year after the ships went down, however. Charles Davieaux, the lighthouse keeper on Michipicoten Island, found a body washed up on the beach. He buried it without the kind of official inquiry and forensic testing we have today, and no one knows whether it came from the two French ships. A skeleton found years later near the little fishing village of Coldwell, on the north shore of Lake Superior, was buried in an unmarked grave. Some people in Coldwell thought the bones may have belonged to one of the French sailors, but Lake Superior takes many lives every year. The wrecks have never been found.

Seven years after the loss of the *Inkerman* and the *Cerisoles*, the Superior Shoal was finally charted near the main steamship course on Lake Superior. It is the peak of an old volcanic hill. Fishermen knew it was there, but kept it a secret. Speculation has continued since the shoal was found that the two minesweepers were lost on it, although there is no more evidence pointing to Superior Shoal than there is to any other spot on the Great Lakes.

The real cause of their loss won't be known until the wrecks are found. Until then, the secrecy of wartime hampers normal speculation. Conspiracy theorists in Thunder Bay believe the ships steamed straight to the United States as part of some secret wartime deal.

Even stranger than the actual sinking, perhaps, was the behavior of the captain of the *Sebastopol*. Why hadn't he reported the loss of the *Inkerman* and the *Cerisoles* when he locked through at Sault Ste. Marie? If he believed the two ships were still afloat and the fleet had simply been separated, why didn't he wait for the other two minesweepers under his command before heading down Lake Huron? Or, if he suspected the loss of the two ships while he was still on Lake Superior, why didn't he begin a search? And why did his telegram from Port Colborne to Fort William, sent at least a week after the loss of the *Inkerman* and *Cerisoles*, not even mention the two lost ships and the eighty men aboard them? Wartime haste may have been a factor in Leclerc's behavior. His actions may have been those of a man who had not yet gained respect for the Great Lakes. After all, he may have believed ocean warships built with watertight compartments could not possibly be threatened by a storm on an inland lake, hundreds of miles from the sea.

And there's one last clue, or red herring, depending on your level of skepticism. It is the handwritten entry in the old, worn, leather-and-corduroy-bound ledger used in those days by the government of Canada to record the nation's shipwrecks. Each wreck is listed alphabetically, by year, with a few details of the wreck, the name of the investigator who led the inquiry into the sinking, and the crewman, if any, who could be blamed for the loss. There are no details about the sinking of the *Inkerman* and the *Cerisoles*. There was no official inquiry. Their loss is simply recorded with a one-line statement. And the grim ledger, now kept in a National Archives of Canada warehouse outside of Ottawa, says they sank on Lake Ontario.

CHAPTER TEN

The Christmas Tree Ships

A LITTLE MORE THAN A CENTURY AGO, the "traditional" trappings of North American-style Christmas would have puzzled most of the people who actually lived in America. Santa Claus was still a wandering saint who traveled the world with his rather nasty sidekick, Black Peter, and dished out joy or punishment to little Dutch and German kids on St. Nicholas Day, December 6. The Dutch version of the story, familiar to people in upstate New York, ended up bowdlerized and transformed in the poem "The Night Before Christmas." Then, in the hands of graphic artists working for a soda pop company, St. Nicholas lost his bishop's miter and Black Peter was written out of the story altogether. Today, Coca

Cola still owns the rights to the image that we think of as Santa Claus.

Christmas trees, too, have evolved from a German Christmas tradition to a mainstream must-have. Christmas trees, or the idea of bringing an evergreen into the home in winter, probably predates Christianity. The ancient Britons were enthralled with holly because it stayed green through the dismal winter days. The Christmas tree, a mix of greenery and light, gives hope that winter's drabness will end and spring's light and greenery will return.

The Christmas tree was a long-established decoration in Germany when German settlers and Revolutionary War Hessian soldiers brought it to America. In those days, Christmas wasn't celebrated with special gusto. In New England, it wasn't celebrated at all. Boston public schools remained open on Christmas day as late as the 1870s, a legacy of the Puritans, who had banned the holiday altogether. As for the Christmas tree, it was greeted with some measure of antipathy: in 1851, a Cleveland minister had to fight to save his job after bringing one into his church. That same year, the Christmas tree business began in New York City, when a farmer arrived with a load from the Catskills. Soon, small, shrubby trees were shipped into New York from logged-over areas upstate and in New England. Still, the custom caught on slowly: by the turn of that century, just one in five American homes had a Christmas tree. It wasn't until the 1920s that the Christmas tree could be said to have come into its own. By then, nearly everyone had one and Christmas had replaced Easter as the most-anticipated holiday in the Christian calendar.

World War I veterans may have helped to spread the

custom. In 1914, German troops on the western front were supplied with small Christmas trees by their quartermasters. The soldiers lit candles on them and placed the little trees on the front edges of the trenches. The lighting of the trees sparked an unofficial truce along most of the front that lasted in some places for a month. Germans met British and French soldiers, traded food and souvenirs (even, to the great consternation of officers, their rifles), and, some writers claim, even played soccer.

Clampdowns in succeeding Christmases put an end to the truces, but the event had been reported in the world's largest newspapers as a sign that some humanity still existed in a world where decency, order, and sanity had broken down. When U.S. troops arrived at the western front in 1917, there were still some veterans who regaled them with the story of the trees in the trenches. In 1917, Halifax, Nova Scotia, was flattened by the explosion of the munitions ship *Mont Blanc*. Citizens of Boston organized a special train to take relief supplies and doctors to the shattered city, an act of kindness that has been repaid every year since with Halifax's gift to Boston of a Christmas tree.

Anyone wanting to experience the joy of Christmas trees could easily have found a home with a tree in Chicago. The practice of keeping one had jumped from the large German community to the rest of the city's families in the 1880s. At the same time, Chicago developed a tradition of its own: the Christmas tree ships. Tens of thousands of trees were brought to the city each year between 1880 and the early 1920s by means that were particularly risky.

At its height, the trade may have drawn in as many as sixty ships, although in any one year, no more than about a dozen entered Chicago harbor. Collecting and shipping Christmas trees on Lake Michigan began just after the Civil War. In 1875, the first Christmas tree ship to meet disaster set out for the northern Michigan town of Boyne City. The *Caledonia*, a leaky and dilapidated schooner, was loaded with trees by her owner Hans Peterson and his two-man crew. The ship cleared the harbor breakwater, and was plodding through Traverse Bay, when it developed a massive leak. At 5:00 A.M. that cold December morning, the crew took to the lifeboat. They made it just in time to see the *Caledonia* capsize. A steamer picked up the nearly frozen men a day later and dropped them off, broke but alive, at Milwaukee.

In the late 1890s, word that captains on the East Coast were making good money by bringing trees down to Boston and New York from Canada and Maine spurred their counterparts on the Great Lakes to keep trying. August and Hermann Schuenemann, whose parents had immigrated to northern Wisconsin just before the Civil War, knew that the region was full of Christmas trees. Millions of small evergreens grew in logged-over places and in areas hit by a massive forest fire in 1871. The Schuenemanns were entrepreneurs, although not, perhaps, especially prosperous ones. They bought old schooners for the Christmas tree trade at bankruptcy sales, and then found down-on-their-luck sailors to work on them. As young men, they shifted their home from Algoma, Wisconsin to the North Side of Chicago and, by the turn of the century their Christmas tree lot at the Clark Street bridge was a Christmas landmark.

The Schuenemanns went into the Christmas tree business in 1876. Their schooner, the *W.H. Hinsdale* took a load of 1,300 Christmas trees from Algoma to Chicago in

December, but, the next spring, the boat was wrecked at South Haven, Michigan. August Schuenemann had been in command and survived the sinking. For a few hundred dollars, there were still schooners for sale along the lake. Steam ships had made them obsolete.

The Schuenemanns soon had competition. In 1877, Captain John McDonald went into the trade, using his fishing schooner to try to make a few dollars at the end of the season. To make the best profits, captains had to time their arrival in Chicago perfectly. They had to unload early, before the main rush, but not so early that their trees dried out before people were smitten by the Christmas spirit. Captain McDonald arrived too late one year, showing up at Chicago harbor with a load of trees that no one wanted. The Milwaukee *Sentinel*, in December, 1888, described the business:

> The trade is carried on mainly by small country store-keepers located near a harbor or railway station. The farmers in their vicinity or the woodsmen, who buy all their articles of food, clothing, etc., from these stores, make their payments in Christmas trees. Some farmers would like to buy Christmas presents for their wives, children, relatives, or friends, but they are short in cash, or hate to part with it. Near their farms are acres of marsh land covered with pines and shrubbery. They ask the store-keeper whether trees would be acceptable to him in lieu of money. The store-keeper consents, and in a few days carloads of Christmas trees are piled up near his house. He engages a few workmen and has the crude pine branches properly shaped, and then he begins to

ship them south. Thus is this peculiar trade carried on
throughout the entire northern part of the peninsula.
The trees are shipped not alone to Milwaukee. All the
cities of this state and hundreds of cities and hamlets in
Illinois are supplied with them, and certainly one-half of
the Christmas trees sold in Chicago come from the
Badger state.

Milwaukee's own large German community was also a good
market for Christmas trees, which arrived early in December
on schooners that picked them up at the north end of Green
Bay and in Michigan. By the end of the century, the demand
was so great that Christmas tree ship captains had to hunt
for cargo in Lake Huron and, in the glory days, even gathered them along the coast of Lake Superior. By then, the
railways had joined in. Competition drove prices up in the
hinterland and down in the city, so captains like the
Schuenemanns had to come up with cost-cutting ideas and
find ways of making more money from the trees.

The ships employed in the trade, unsafe to begin with,
were even more dangerously neglected. The trees were
crammed into the holds below and piled high on the decks
above. The fire risk was obvious. As well, the ships were vulnerable to ice that accumulated on the trees from spray or
freezing rain. Booms had to be raised, sailors had to climb
over the rigging, and the ships handled very poorly in any
kind of weather. Some sailors, seeing a loaded Christmas
tree ship, refused to board. In at least one case, a man hired
by the Schuenemanns hid on the dock among cargo crates
rather than board one of their ships. The ownership of the
ships was complicated, possibly to evade liability. The

Schuenemanns acted as though they knew the trade was risky. Ships were registered in wives' names. Secret ownership and partnership rules were made. Even now, it's difficult to tell which ships the family owned and which were part of complicated, and possibly illegal, deals.

It was only a matter of time before a disaster occurred. August Schuenemann commanded the schooner *S. Thal* in December, 1898, as she carried a load of Christmas trees from Wisconsin to Chicago. The *Thal* was hit broadside by a fast-moving storm. Better ships than the *Thal* ran into trouble in that December blast. People living along the shore near Winnetka were puzzled to observe that the *Thal* was flying its flag at half-mast. (If the ship were in trouble, observers would expect to see the flag flown upside-down.) Later, the crew of the ship seemed to have recovered control, but, by late afternoon, as the *Thal* tried to steer for the mouth of the Chicago River, the wind tore its old sails to shreds. The *Thal* was tossed by the waves for a few hours before being wrecked on a sandbar south of the city, taking August Schuenemann and his two-man crew with her. The wreck, if anything still held together, was never found, nor were the bodies of the men on board. Proof of the destruction of the *Thal*—a plank with her name on it—washed ashore the next spring near the Illinois–Indiana line.

Despite the loss, the Schuenemanns stayed in the tree business. Now, with the need to support August's widow and children, the family had to find more ways of squeezing money out of the business. The Schuenemann hulks worked the main shipping season carrying any freight available, and charging discount prices for doing it. Once the Christmas tree season started, the women of the family served customers at the Clark Street bridge Christmas tree lot. In their spare moments, they wove discarded Christmas tree branches into wreaths that they sold for a few cents each. When the family found that they could no longer low-ball the lumbermen along the Lake Michigan shore, they began buying trees from Ojibwa Indians at the Soo. And, when they had enough money, they bought some logged-over land in Wisconsin, and let nature grow trees for them. The Schuenemanns traveled north every fall with a group of down-and-out laborers who cut the trees at rock-bottom prices.

The Schuenemanns' arrival became a Chicago tradition. There was no longer a race between them and other captains. They undercut all their competitors. Nor did they sell off their stock to wholesalers. Instead, they developed what business professors call a vertically integrated company, one that controlled the trade from production to final sale. However, the lynchpin of the operation was a handful of ships, some of them pushing eighty years old, that were in such sad shape that the brothers could snap them up for the cost of their rigging. Two years before his brother drowned, Hermann had a close call when one of his boats ran aground and fell apart. Hermann himself would have been in the storm that claimed his brother if he hadn't stayed home to be with his wife for the birth of their twin daughters.

"Christmas Tree Schuenemann" came each year to the same spot at the southwest corner of the bridge. Nearby, one of his ships, tied to a pier, was strung with electric lights from mast to mast. A big sign read "Christmas Tree Ship. My Prices Are the Lowest." In the busy season, the women of the family slept in the cabin of the ship. Besides making

The Rouse Simmons *had seen better days by the time the* Schuenemanns *took her over.*

wreaths, they dealt with the public, priced the trees, and decided which of the biggest and best would be offered to the grand hotels along Michigan Avenue.

There were many omens of what was to happen, but Hermann Schuenemann chose not to read them. A more sensitive man probably would have dropped out of the business, or at least been much more attentive to safety after the death of his brother. In 1897 he bought the schooner *Mary Collins.* Three years later, she fell apart at the south end of the lake, near Manistique, Michigan. His next ship was the lumber schooner *Truman Moss.* In 1903 Hermann bought the schooner *George L. Wrenn,* the biggest ship he ever owned. He paid just $377.68 for the 129-foot, three-masted ship, a suspiciously small amount. In 1906 the Manistique *Courier-Record* described the *Wrenn* in less-than-glowing terms: "The boat's hull is in good condition below the waterline but her rigging and upper works are a sorry sight." She was no longer used in the general freight or lumber business. The Christmas tree runs became a one-shot deal. The rest of the time, the schooner was tied up, decay taking its toll.

Hermann Schuenemann, who spent most of the year scouting tree-growing areas, pruning trees on his own land, and caulking his ships, hired other captains to sail them. He understood the focus of his business had changed. His business cards, by 1910, read "Northern Michigan Evergreen Nursery" and his working address was described as "Southwest Corner Clark Street Bridge." He also leased a few old schooners to handle some of the trade. The schooner *Rouse Simmons* was one such boat. She had been built in the early 1870s and named for her owner, the founder of the Simmons Mattress Company. In her day, she had been a fine vessel, but that time had long past when Schuenemann began leasing her in the fall of 1910.

In 1911 the *Rouse Simmons*, heading north, was trapped by a storm off Two Rivers Point. The delay was another omen. Two Rivers Point was the place where Hermann ran aground in 1895. He had yet another appointment with the place in 1912.

That fall, Schuenemann took the *Rouse Simmons* north and loaded her with some 5,000 trees. Sailing home with a crew of seventeen (probably most of them laborers who cut and loaded the trees), he ran into a violent storm. People at Kewaunee saw the Simmons flying her flag upside down, but no one there braved the storm to assist it. A rescue crew at Two Rivers Point made ready to head out into the lake in their gasoline-powered boat, but the *Simmons* never sailed by. At about 3:00 P.M. on November 23, the *Simmons* went to the bottom of Lake Michigan, taking Hermann Schuenemann with her.

Years later, a bottle washed ashore in Sheboygan, Wisconsin. Inside was a note: "Friday.... everybody good-bye. I guess we are all through. During the night the small boat washed overboard. Leaking bad. Invald and Steve lost too. God help us." Schuenemann's wallet was found on the far side of the lake.

Wreckage, including hundreds of Christmas trees, washed up along the west shore of the lake. For years, trees were spotted by lake sailors and were caught in commercial fishermen's nets, grim reminders of the passing of the *Simmons*, her crew, and Captain Schuenemann. The wreck of the most famous Christmas tree ship was found in 1971 off Two Rivers Point by Milwaukee diver G. Kent Bellrichard. It's now a popular dive spot.

As for the Christmas tree ships, they were off the lakes by the late 1920s, but today the Coast Guard brings a load into Chicago by cutter every fall and distributes trees to poorer children. The Christmas tree ships are celebrated in songs, plays, and television shows in Chicago, and their legend is part of the city's Christmas lore.

It took more than ten days for word of the sinking of the *Simmons* to reach Chicago. The tragedy was front-page news. "Christmas Tree Ship Lost" ran the headline of the Chicago *American*. "Find Wreckage, Fear Christmas Boat Sunk," the *Daily News* announced. "Santa Claus Ship and Thirteen Lost in Lake," proclaimed the Chicago *Journal*.

A few newspapers, like the Grand Haven *Daily Tribune* of December 3, 1912, told readers Schuenemann might

have been at least partly responsible for his own death and
the loss of his ship and crew:

> The old schooner *Rouse Simmons*, for which fears were
> felt, is the same craft which a few years ago was picked
> up in mid-lake one late fall day in a badly water-logged
> condition by the car ferry *Grand Haven*. The ferry was
> bound from Grand Haven to Milwaukee in a heavy sea,
> when a craft was sighted ahead with a distress signal fly-
> ing from her lone spar. She was low in the water and
> seemed in instant danger of sinking. Huddled together
> on the deck house, just out of reach of the sea, and
> drenched with the flying spray, was the crew of the ship.
>
> Recognizing their plight, Captain Lyman, who then
> commanded the *Grand Haven*, headed the big ship
> directly for the water-logged craft. After several attempts
> he succeeded in getting a line to the schooner and tow-
> ing her into Milwaukee, where she arrived safely. That
> day came near seeing the end of the *Rouse Simmons*, and
> now after being several days overdue in a series of terrible
> blows she has again turned up safely.

That near-disaster happened before Shuenemann leased the
Simmons, but a man who sailed the lakes for forty years
should have recognized a deathtrap when he saw it.

The surviving Schuenemanns were caught in a trap of
their own. The Christmas tree season of 1912 went down
with Hermann Schuenemann. There was no insurance: no
company would touch the ship and its cargo, even if
Hermann Schuenemann had been willing to pay an under-
writer. That year, the surviving Schuenemanns were able to

scrape up trees from other captains and use Hermann's modest assets as seed money for a corner store. For twenty years, until her death in 1930, Schuenemann's widow sold trees on a lot at 1641 North LaSalle Street. Even after her death, the three surviving Schuenemann daughters kept selling wreaths and trees until, in 1932, a time when the city's teachers and police endured "payless paydays" and almost all of the city's industry lay idle, the women gave the last of their trees away to poor families living west of Clark Street.

CHAPTER ELEVEN

Unsafe at Any Speed

"Are you all set and ready for the big
event? A long time ago Jonah took a trip on a whale.
There is no Jonah about this, but it will be a Whale of a
Success. Get your tickets early. Adults 75 cents.
Children under five free! Children between
five and twelve, half fare!"

JONAH SURVIVED his trip in a whale, but, for more
than 800 passengers on the excursion ship *Eastland*, the
tickets to the "big event" advertised for July 24, 1915—
an excursion out of the hot city of Chicago to the
dune-lined beaches of Michigan City, Indiana—was an invi-
tation to die.

The *Eastland* should have been in a scrap yard. She had
been built to carry both freight and passengers out of her
home port of South Haven. There's a sandbar across the

mouth of South Haven's harbor, so the *Eastland* was designed to travel fully loaded in just twelve feet of water.

The Sydney Jenks shipyard in South Haven had very little experience building passenger ships. In the *Eastland*, they originally planned a ship that was both fast and comfortable. With a length of 265 feet and a breadth of just thirty-eight feet, she would be two feet narrower than the sleekest of ships then sailing on the Great Lakes. Then they decided to shorten the ship and add an extra deck. This extra deck accentuated the ship's design flaws. She was powered by two 3,500-horsepower, triple-expansion engines that drove twin propellers.

The *Eastland*'s fatal flaw was the builders' and owners' belief that the *Eastland* would always carry freight. When a full load of cargo was packed into the hold of the ship, her metacentric height—the ship's center of gravity—was fairly low. Passengers prefer the higher points on ships, well above the center of gravity, so the cargo below the waterline was needed for ballast. As it turned out, the *Eastland* rarely carried much cargo, but she was popular with tourists, who had no idea that they were sailing on a ship that rode far too high in the water.

And there were other problems. The four gangways were low. They tended to act a bit like levers tipping the boat on its side as the tons of people and baggage were loaded and unloaded. When the *Eastland* was loaded to capacity, these gangways were just twelve inches above the waterline. Sometimes, when the gangways were crowded, the *Eastland* listed so far that water lapped onto the deck.

The men who sailed her quickly understood that the *Eastland* had problems. In her early years, one cabin deck was removed. This helped to stabilize the *Eastland* when she had a relatively small load of passengers, but, on busy trips, many of them climbed to the flat upper deck to enjoy the view. The answer would have been to build a promenade deck much lower on the ship, but the owners preferred to try less expensive fixes.

To compensate for the weight of the passengers, twelve ballast tanks were built into the ship's lower hull. The tanks were slow to fill and had no gauge. The chief engineer had to rely on experience and the feel of the ship to adjust the ship's trim. The system was actually designed to lighten the ship so it could navigate the shallow river harbors on southern Lake Michigan and to give it a lower draft for the open lake. They were also used to offset the list that developed when the *Eastland* was loaded and unloaded. The ballast system might have worked if people hadn't moved around on the decks, but this was not the case. Most of the Eastland's passengers were day-trippers, who either stood or wandered around the *Eastland* over the course of their outing. Often they moved as a mass to one side of the ship or the other to see anything of interest on the shore or lake.

And there were other problems: extra mechanical equipment was built into the *Eastland* in her first decade, and then a heavy air conditioning system was installed in the upper decks. In 1914, nearly fifty tons of concrete were added to the decks to try to stabilize her. Finally, on July 2, 1915, three heavy lifeboats and six rafts were added to the weight of the superstructure. This addition was ironic: it was inspired by the *Titanic* tragedy three years earlier. The extra lifeboats were meant to make the *Eastland* safer.

There were warnings that the *Eastland* would capsize, if anyone wanted to listen. William Wood, a marine engineer hired in 1903 to fix the *Eastland's* problems, said she was "the crank of the lakes and as far as I know, the only crank of the lakes." It was he who recommended the removal of the upper deck. Even then, he warned: "The design of the vessel would not permit its operation as other vessels are operated and great care had to be taken at all times." In August, 1906, after a series of near-mishaps, the *Eastland*, carrying 2,530 passengers in the middle of Lake Michigan, listed so badly that a formal complaint was filed with marine authorities and some passengers took their stories to the Chicago newspapers. The ship's owners countered by placing advertisements in two Chicago papers offering a $5,000 reward to anyone who could prove the *Eastland* was unsafe. They ignored the letters written by marine engineers who, almost every year, reported to federal authorities that the *Eastland* should be taken out of service.

The chief obstacle faced by the *Eastland's* detractors was the fact that she was a beautiful and popular ship. During a short, previous career based in Cleveland, she had been one of the busiest excursion ships on Lake Erie. She was fast and sleek, possessed a large dance floor, and carried a good orchestra. She was a consistent hit with day-trippers. After returning from her daily cruise, the *Eastland* was loaded with passengers at twenty-five cents a head for an evening trip. Couples danced in the cool night breezes on the moon-lit deck, while landlubbers made special trips to the shore just to watch the *Eastland* sail by. She was lit from bow to stern, and the strains of waltzes or the latest foxtrots drifted across the water. Sailors on incoming ore freighters said the

Eastland's floating party was so tempting that they wanted to dive overboard and swim to her.

In July, 1915, the world was gripped by war. The U.S. was still neutral but, that spring, the great Cunard liner *Lusitania* was torpedoed by a German U-boat off the Irish coast with the loss of 1,198 passengers and crew. The attack did not draw the U.S. into the war, but the country's factories were running flat-out to supply war materiel to the American armed forces and the Western allies. Factory workers in Chicago worked six days a week in that hot summer. For employees of the Western Electric Company, one of the largest and best employers in the city, the annual summer picnic was a much-needed and longed-for break.

The morning of July 24 was gray and drizzly as Harry Pedersen, captain of the *Eastland*, made his ship ready for the Western Electric excursion. At 3:00 A.M. the ship entered the Chicago River and headed for the Chicago and South Haven Wharf. Dawn broke just before 6:00 A.M. and, already, thousands of people waited at the *Eastland*'s berth on the south side of the river between LaSalle and Clark streets. At about this time, First Assistant Engineer Charles Silvernail and his assistant, Fred Snow, began pumping out the ballast tanks.

At 6:30 A.M., the *Eastland*'s four gangways were rolled onto the wharf and immediately hundreds of people began streaming onto the ship. They arrived on the deck at a rate of about one per second. Within ten minutes of the first passengers' boarding, a noticeable list to starboard began worrying the ship's officers. First Engineer Joseph Erickson ordered the engine room crew to steady the ship. Valves on the ballast tanks were opened for two or three minutes. The

Eastland straightened and, for two minutes, the ship seemed balanced. Then she began listing to port (toward the center of the river). Again, ballast tanks were flooded and the ship steadied herself. Tugs were dispatched to tow the *Eastland* to the harbor. At 7:00 A.M., the tug *Kenosha* arrived and took up position at the *Eastland*'s bow.

Harbormaster Adam F. Weckler arrived at the Clark Street bridge just after the *Kenosha* took up her position and was horrified to see the *Eastland* listing at about seven degrees. He ordered boarding to stop. The *Eastland* was already at capacity, with about 2,500 people on her decks, but more people tried to crowd on board. Crew members on the *Eastland*, like radio operator Charles M. Dibbell, tried to get passengers to spread out on the *Eastland*'s decks. Most ignored this advice. They congregated on the port side and aft along the promenade deck, where they could hear Bradfield's Orchestra, which had just started playing. Many passengers began dancing.

By 7:15, Erickson was very worried. The list had more than doubled in the past ten minutes. He ordered more ballast tanks to be flooded, and, yet again, the *Eastland* righted herself. The Clark Street Bridge was blocked so it could be raised. Crew members started to cast off the lines for both the *Eastland* and *Kenosha*. Western Electric worker E.W. Sladkey, who arrived late, stood on the wharf and noticed the list to port. He decided to board another ship but, as he turned away, co-workers called to him to jump aboard. He made the short leap across the water, becoming the last of the passengers to arrive on the *Eastland*'s crowded deck.

At that moment, water began rolling over the *Eastland*'s deck and into the hold. Bottles and broken glass tumbled across the main deck as sailors tried to get the passengers to move away from the railings. Chief Steward Albert Wycoff was in the lunchroom on the main deck when he noticed the boat listing. "Dishes fell off the rack and a scene of wild excitement followed."

By now, most sailors knew the ship was taking on water. Snow, seeing water flood into the hold from a gangway hatch, set off a warning signal to the bridge. Pedersen ignored it and radioed for the Clark Street Bridge to be raised. Weckler, the harbormaster, refused, saying the *Eastland* had to be straightened before it could leave the berth. The ship was straining on the last of its mooring ropes.

At least some sailors realized that the *Eastland*, now with a 25-degree list, was doomed. Captain Pedersen, however, wouldn't accept the evidence before his own eyes. His men were already fleeing from the boiler room as he walked the decks demanding the last lines be cast off. The stern of the *Eastland* had drifted a few yards into the river, but the bow was still tied to the wharf.

The musicians in Bradfield's Orchestra realized the ship was in trouble. Like the *Titanic's* dance band, they braced themselves on the tilting deck, and struck up a lively ragtime tune. Passengers were still calm. Outwardly, the crew appeared to be in control of the situation. Few of the Western Electric employees and their relatives noticed the engine crew had joined them on the deck. A moment later, just as dishes in the dining room were tumbling from their racks, the piano on the promenade deck broke loose, rolled across the floor, and trapped a grocer, Charles Bender, who drowned under it when the ship capsized. The refrigerators at the bar toppled over, trapping two women. That was the signal to panic.

As the port side of the ship rose higher into the air, passengers instinctively climbed higher into the *Eastland's* decks, increasing the ship's instability, and setting themselves up to be trapped when she rolled over. Water streamed through open portholes. The port side and most of the cabin area rolled underwater while passengers jumped from the starboard side, landing on the wharf or in the river. Those who leaped from the bow or the stern had the best chance of survival. Passengers on the starboard, or land, side had a reasonable possibility of escape, but those on the port side were doomed. Few people had life jackets and the only person to be saved by the ship's lifeboats was a six-year-old boy who climbed into one as it drifted on the river.

Chicago *Herald* reporter Harlan E. Babcock arrived at the wharf expecting to travel to Michigan City with the crowd of holidaymakers and write a feel-good story about the day. Instead, he watched from the pier as the ship capsized:

I vaguely remembered having heard that the *Eastland* had been condemned some years ago and I felt that the crew was taking awful chances in overcrowding the boat, especially as the vessel kept listing gradually but more and more every minute toward the river. Then a tugboat steamed alongside and gave several deep-throated blasts, which evidently was the signal to cast off and start. But it never cast off. Before even the crew had time to release the hawsers that held the boat to the dock, the vessel began to topple, and in less time than it takes to tell it, the sight of that horror stricken throng of thousands, the

Eastland...careened, hurling hundreds screaming into
the black waters of the river.

A story in that day's *Herald* described the scene that ensued:

> The mad scramble, a panic in which the terrified passen-
> gers fought for places of safety. Shrieks and cries wrung
> the hearts of those on shore. A minute or two more and
> the ship was flat on its side...and those caught beneath
> and within were entombed. The surface of the river was
> thick with struggling forms. Babies perished in sight of
> those on the docks and bridges.

Captain Pederson easily survived by pulling himself
onto the pilothouse. Erickson climbed through an air duct
and out a porthole. In fact, most of the *Eastland*'s crew got
out alive. Probably, over the years, the wiser ones had made
their plans for just such an emergency. Chief Steward
Wycoff "shouted for the people to save themselves. A
moment later I jumped into the water and managed to rescue three women."

Later that day, one crew member, L.D. Gadery, "candy
butcher" on the *Eastland,* told a reporter of his escape:

> It was about 7:40 in the morning and the boat was lying
> at the dock near Clark Street Bridge loading with passen-
> gers. We were to leave in twenty minutes and the upper
> decks and cabins were crowded with passengers. There
> were hundreds of women and children. I estimate there
> were between 2,000 and 3,000 passengers on the boat at
> the time of the accident. I was standing on the lower

deck near the gangplank watching the people come aboard. Suddenly I noticed the boat list toward the center of the river. It rolled slightly at first, then seemed to stop. Then it started to roll again. I became alarmed and shouted at the crowd to keep still. Apparently a majority of the crowd was on one side of the boat and this had over-weighted it and caused it to list. Suddenly the hawsers that held the ship to the dock snapped and the officers pulled the gangplank in and refused to allow any more on the boat.

At this time, everyone was panic-stricken. Women screamed and men tried to quiet them. I attempted to reach an upper deck but could not because of the crowd and the excitement, and ran back to the port side where the gangplank had been. The boat then began to slowly drift away from the dock, rolling as it slipped into midstream and a moment later it turned over on its side. I climbed over onto the side of the boat and stayed there until I was taken off by lifesavers. Many of the passengers leaped into the water as the boat went over. Scores of others were caught in the cabins and drowned. When the small boats began coming out to us I worked with other survivors to take passengers out of the water and cutting holes in the cabins to remove bodies.

Policeman Henry Sesher, who watched the horror from the wharf, saw scores of men and women, many of them holding children, plunge into the water:

I jumped into a rowboat and pulled out the drowning. I think I got about fifty ashore. The fireboat and tugs hurried to the scene and picked up more than a hundred people. We grabbed those nearest to us. At one time, I had four women in the boat with me. Others I aided by dragging them from the water onto the docks.

Passenger Emma O'Donnell said the *Eastland* never stopped when it started to roll, "and a few moments [later] it was out in the middle of the river on its side. I saw dozens of people drown around me but was unable to give assistance." She clawed her way out of the promenade deck, crawled along the side of the ship, and clutched the wreck of the *Eastland* until she was taken off by rescuers three hours later. The 1,700 survivors swam in the river among the bodies of the dead or huddled on the wharf in shock. Gretchen Krohn was on the pier when the *Eastland* rolled over. She described the scene when, at noon, rescue workers pulled the living and the dead from the wreck:

> Up the slippery wet side canvas was spread that those carrying out the bodies might bring out their gruesome freight at a dog trot and thus empty the overturned basketful of human beings more quickly. All of the bodies carried past were so rigid that poles to carry them seemed superfluous. And the pitiful shortness of most of them! Children, and yet more children. And when it wasn't a child, it was a young girl of 18 or so.

Charles Agnastoklio (Agnos) had been looking forward to the company picnic—he was one of the first people aboard. He sensed from the beginning that there was something wrong. He stayed on the ship and, when it rolled, was able to get out on deck and ride on the superstructure as the *Eastland* capsized:

> The top remained above water. I didn't even get wet—at
> first. Suddenly, I was hit by scrambling people and
> dumped into the river. I drank that Chicago river water
> and—ooohhh—it was bad. Those of us who drank the
> water were treated for possible diseases with shots. I
> found my way out of the ship by vents, passageways, and
> I don't know what all.

The panic in the water was mirrored by a near-riot at the pier and the Clark Street Bridge. The hundreds of screaming people in the water clawed at each other as they tried to find a way to safety. A few level-headed policemen and sailors threw life jackets into the struggling mass, but hundreds of people, mostly children, drowned within a few feet of shore. Some rescuers went aboard the *Eastland* and used fire axes to chop holes in the wooden walls of the cabin decks to free trapped passengers.

Two days after the tragedy, Bert Cross, who was one of the Western Electric employees who escaped from the *Eastland* that Saturday morning, wrote to his mother:

> Even when [the *Eastland*] was leaning at a 45-degree
> angle the women and girls were laughing and joking and
> were not aware of any danger. And then the boat turned
> over and the fight for life began. I don't know yet how I
> managed to get out on the side of the ship. And for the
> next two hours I worked pulling men, women and little
> children out of the boat and from the water. If I live to

be a thousand years old I will never forget the experience.

The whole river was a mass of struggling humanity, when hundreds were drowning before my eyes. You have probably read about it in the papers but no one can picture the horror of the scene. Men and women covered with blood from broken windows, children and girls struggling in the water calling for help and the people trapped within the boat who never had a chance for their life. The ones in the water were soon recovered if they were alive, but in the cabins, staterooms and on the lower decks it was hours before the steel plates could be cut into and their bodies taken out. I didn't mind so much the pulling out of people who were alive but when we commenced to pull up dead ones, little girls and boys and even babies strapped in go-carts, then I quit, I couldn't stand it any longer.

By 8:00 A.M., all of the survivors were pulled from the river. Ashes from the fireboxes of the tugboats were scattered on the side of the wreck to give rescuers some traction. A few more survivors emerged from the wreck over the course of the afternoon but, as evening approached, the rescue had become a body-recovery operation.

Nets were thrown across the river at several points downstream to catch the corpses. Divers checked the nets every few minutes while stricken family members waited on the pier for news. Grown men standing by the docks wept as the dead were pulled from the river or from the hold of the ship. Women, especially mothers of lost children waiting for news, collapsed under the strain or became inconsolable.

As word of the tragedy spread, ships from around the Great Lakes joined the rescue effort. Local businesses were also generous in providing aid. The Commonwealth Edison Company donated 125 tungsten-nitrogen lights, which were set up on the starboard side of the *Eastland* and on the nearby Reid Murdoch Building to illuminate the wharf area so the rescuers could see as they worked through the night. Two days later, a diving tug, the *Favorite,* pulled up to the wharf and was used as a headquarters for the divers. Special lights built into the bottom of the *Favorite* helped the divers see in the murky water.

Meanwhile, citizens of the horrified city looked for people to blame. The city coroner ordered the arrest of every official of the Illinois Transportation Company, the *Eastland*'s owners. W. C. Steele, secretary-treasurer of the St. Joseph-Chicago steamship company, the ship's previous owner, was also lodged in the cells of a police station, along with the *Eastland*'s captain, first mate, and twenty-seven other members of her crew.

Before he was arrested, Captain Pederson held an impromptu press conference on the pier and tried to deflect blame by claiming ignorance of the ship's instability: "The cause is a mystery to me," he told reporters a few minutes before he was taken to jail. "I have sailed the lakes for twenty-five years, and before that sailed the ocean for twelve years, and this is the first serious accident I've ever had. I do not know how it happened." Other experts ridiculed the captain's defense. U.S. Coast Guard Lieutenant Commander Eric Christensen told the Chicago *Tribune*, "The *Eastland* was an accident waiting to happen."

The recriminations gave cold comfort to the families of

the dead. Most were people of modest means who had recently arrived in America. As the corpses arrived on the pier, they had to be identified, a difficult process since there were no passenger lists. The city morgue was quickly filled and temporary morgues were set up in warehouses along the river. The largest temporary morgue was in the Reid-Murdock building at the wreck site. The Second Regiment Armory on Washington Boulevard was established as the central morgue. There, the bodies that were unidentified were laid out in rows. At midnight of the day of the tragedy, the doors were opened and the families of the missing passengers filed in to look for their loved ones.

At the local cemeteries, foremen supervised hundreds of volunteer gravediggers. Delivery trucks were used as hearses. Churches held funerals for as many as thirty bodies at a time. The death toll was 844 men, women, and children. Only two were members of the *Eastland*'s crew, and one was a man who died in the rescue effort. Although 1,523 had died on the *Titanic*, the more famous ship actually had a lower death toll of passengers. Crew deaths in the *Titanic* disaster totalled 694.

Chicago's Mayor William Hale Thompson was at the San Francisco Panama-Pacific Exposition's Illinois Day when the *Eastland* capsized. He hurried back to Chicago on a special train while Acting Mayor Moorhouse organized a fundraising drive to collect $200,000 to help the families of the victims and to bury the dead. Western Electric was the largest donor, giving the relief drive $100,000.

On the afternoon of the tragedy, President Woodrow Wilson sent a telegram to Mayor Thompson: "I am sure I speak the universal feeling of the people of the country in expressing my profound sympathy and sorrow in the presence of the great disaster which saddened so many homes."

Kind words and charity were not enough to ease the pain of the city. While the ship's officers and owners waited in jail, newspapers hinted that government inspectors were either bribed or in some other way persuaded to allow for the increased passenger loads for the sake of big profits. A story in the Chicago *Herald* quoted Illinois District Attorney Maclay Hoyne saying that members of the U.S. Inspection Bureau were aware that the *Eastland* was unsafe, but they licenced her to carry big passenger loads anyway. "If the inspectors of the bureau had done their duty, the accident could not have occurred. We know the ship was considered unsafe by them, because there are letters on file in Washington which predicted Saturday's occurrence. I have copies of these letters," Hoyne said.

These letters from marine engineers did, in fact, exist. Whether they pointed to graft or conspiracy was another matter. If Hoyne possessed proof of wrongdoing, however, or if it existed in any other file available to prosecutors, it never surfaced in the litigation that lasted for the next twenty years.

An Illinois grand jury leveled indictments charging negligence and manslaughter against Captain Pedersen, Chief Engineer Erickson, two steamboat inspectors, and an official of the Indiana Transportation Company, but a federal judge threw them out for lack of evidence. The charges were then changed to conspiring to operate an unsafe ship, but the accused men were acquitted on those charges. Finally, in August 1935, the United States Circuit Court of Appeals upheld a District Court ruling that the St. Joseph-Chicago Steamship Co. was not liable for the disaster. The court found the company was liable only to the extent of the salvage of the vessel (the usual amount in a marine accident); that the boat was seaworthy; that the operators had taken proper precautions; and that the responsibility was traced to an engineer who neglected to fill the ballast tanks properly. Of the $50,000 that was awarded in the civil lawsuit by the court, about $35,000 went to pay to raise the *Eastland*. The rest went to other creditors. The families received nothing but their small share of the money raised in the 1915 relief drives.

The *Eastland* was, by far, the Great Lakes' worst ship disaster. It has been a part of Chicago's history—Carl Sandburg wrote a poem about it, and a small plaque on the Clark Street Bridge marks the site of the disaster—but it's nearly forgotten everywhere else. Perhaps World War I overshadows it. Maybe it lacks the drama and glamour of the sinking of the *Titanic*. Still, it carried with it a haunting sadness for the families of the dead. Most were new Americans who barely had time to establish themselves in the country. The survivors, the widows, the widowers, and the orphans were left in many cases to make their way alone.

The *Eastland* survived. By the end of the summer, the ship was righted and raised. It was sold to the U.S. Navy for use as a training ship. She was rebuilt and renamed the U.S.S. *Wilmette*, and was mounted with artillery, which she used in 1921 against the only German U-boat sunk in the Great Lakes.

UC-97, a mine-laying submarine, was built at Hamburg, Germany by Blohm & Voss and launched on March 17, 1918. The shipyard was unable to finish the submarine before the Armistice. In early 1919, the UC-97 was delivered to England, as required by the terms of the Armistice, and was one of the six U-boats transferred to the U.S. In March 1919, a navy crew boarded UC-97 and sailed it to the U.S., reaching New York City on April 27. The little U-boat fleet was divided up and the UC-97 was sent to the Great Lakes as a prop for a Victory Bonds campaign. In August, 1919, she arrived in Chicago after a tour of the lakes and was turned over to the Commandant, 9th Naval District. The navy had no need for a U-boat based in Chicago and so, for lack of anything better to do with her, she was laid up at the Great Lakes Naval Station. On June 7, 1921, she was taken out into the open water of Lake Michigan and sunk by the *Eastland*.

Finally, in 1947, the *Eastland* kept her long-overdue appointment with the scrap-yard.

CHAPTER TWELVE

The Convict Ship *Success*

IN THE MIDDLE AGES, an Englishman faced the death penalty for crimes that, in any civilized society, are looked upon as vile: murder; rape; arson of a dwelling house; treason. The rest were dealt with by fines, lashings, imprisonment, or public shaming in the stocks. The British Parliament, as it rose to power 500 years ago, added steadily to the list of capital offences. By the late 1600s, about fifty crimes carried the death penalty. In the century before America's Revolution, another 180 crimes were added to the list. In those same years, and in the decades after the Revolution, Britain's cities grew into metropolises with a huge criminal underclass. Police forces took shape and the jails of England were crammed with the flotsam of society who were fortunate enough to dodge the hangman.

Lawmakers spent neither time nor money on rehabilitation. Those individuals who were convicted but spared the death penalty had to be disposed of cheaply. Some went into the army or the navy, others were stored in rotting prison ships in the harbors of England, and those who were considered most threatening to the state were shipped to the hell of Australia and Tasmania's penal colonies, where they worked as near-slaves with some slight hope of ever regaining their freedom.

Australia's involuntary colonists were a mixed bag: incorrigible thieves from the big cities were shipped out with prostitutes, vagrants, and Irish rebels. Even some Canadian rebels and Americans captured invading Canada and fighting at the Battle of the Windmill during the Rebellion of 1837–38 ended up against their will in the Australasian gulag.

Years later, the descendants of the Patriotes and the Hunters had a chance to gauge the misery that the deportees suffered when the "convict ship" *Success* found her way to the Great Lakes. The 135-foot schooner was an East Indiaman, built of solid teak at Moulmein, Burma, in 1790. For roughly the first fifty years of her existence, she made an honest living trading between England and India. In 1849, she was dispatched to Australia as an immigrant ship, carrying a cargo of paying passengers who wanted a piece of the Australian gold rush. That trip made money for her owners and so, after returning to England, she was sent to Australia again with another load of immigrants. This time, however, her entire crew jumped ship in Melbourne and headed for the gold fields. The captain sold the *Success* to the government of the state of Victoria, which put her to use as a floating prison in Sydney harbor, thus beginning the career for which the *Success* was destined to become notorious.

The Victoria government bought four other ships, in addition to the *Success*, for the same purpose: the *President*, *Lysander*, *Sacramento*, and *Deborah*. These ships soon deteriorated to miserable hulks, their lower decks crammed with tiny cells, and fitted out with restraints, whipping posts, and other hideous fixtures of nineteenth-century prisons. England had used similar prison ships to hold American soldiers captured during the Revolution and as pestilent prisons for its own criminals, but, by the time the *Success* entered the trade, had adopted a slightly more humane penitentiary system.

In fairness, the Australians did have a crime problem. The Australian gold rush was more violent than America's wild west. Outlaws like Ned Kelly (who wore ninety pounds of homemade wrought-iron armor in his criminal escapades), Mad Dan Morgan, Ben Hall, and the Governor Brothers roamed the gold fields and the bush around them. Rather than simply rob banks or hold up stagecoaches, these bandits and their gangs "bailed up" ranches and even entire towns. They would surround their target, cut telegraph wires, and tie up everyone in the place until they had picked it clean. Ned Kelly, who claimed to his last breath that he was forced into crime by the authorities, added to his hostages' pain by making them sit through a 7,000-word sermon on the injustices done to Ned Kelly.

The *Success* became the home to some of these men, including Mad Dan Morgan, who contributed to the ship's grim reputation by leading the attack on John Price, the sadistic supervisor of the floating prisons. Morgan and several other prisoners killed Price with pick-axes while he was overseeing a shore work gang.

The *Success* floated in Kingston harbor for thirty-five years, her miserable cargo never leaving port. Not until 1885 did the authorities decide that they longer needed the prison ships. Some were broken up. Others, including the *Success*, were sold.

A businessman, Alexander Phillips, took possession of the ship in 1890. His plan was to cut the ship down and refashion her as a barge. In the weeks before the work was to begin, however, he and his foreman were mobbed by morbid tourists, so Phillips decided that it would be more profitable to take the *Success* on the road as a kind of popular curiosity. Remarkably, the century-old ship, which had spent thirty-five years at anchor, was still relatively seaworthy. The *Success* sailed first to London, arriving in 1895 fitted out with wax dummies and all of the prison memorabilia her owner could lay hands on, including a set of armor from the Kelly gang. The ship toured Britain's ports for seventeen years. At each stop visitors were charged a few pennies for the privilege of ogling its somewhat horrifying interior.

A writer who toured the *Success* at around this time recorded his impressions:

> No one cannot look upon it without a shudder. She is just as she was left, with cells, instruments, and records complete, and wax figures doing duty for the convicts. Among these figures there is one of Power, the bushranger, who was sentenced to fifteen years' confinement on board; and there is another, somewhat humorously represented as a reformed character and decent member of society, silk hat, and so on, after he had "done his time" and been engaged by the purchasers of the hulk "to be of interest to visitors." Another figure

is that of a black man who served his time and a very rough time—and is now flourishing as a restaurant keeper. There are a few others who seem to have been reformed, but how such treatment could reform any man is a mystery. There are sixty-eight cells in the ship, built along the sides on the main and lower decks, and on each deck is a "tigers' den," a sort of heavily barred loose box, in which the worst characters were herded together.

The dangerous prisoners were on the lower deck, chained in their cells so that they could only just reach the door, the plank near the doorway being in many cases worn into by the prisoner's feet as he waited for the warder to hand him in his bread and water. In some of the cells there is a ring about a yard from the deck, through which the prisoner's arm was passed, so that with the big figure-of-eight handcuffs on he had to kneel or rest against the ship's side, it being impossible for him to stand upright. In the open corridor are the bilboes, in which the prisoner's neck was fastened to an iron bar, while his feet were secured in a kind of stirrups so as to keep him in a stooping posture. The iron work is all appallingly heavy—some of the men had to drag eighty pounds weight about with them—and one of the noteworthy fittings of the ship is a wheel aloft, by means of which a sort of cage was hauled up with the men in it to take an airing, the fetters and manacles being too heavy for them to walk up the stairs with.

In 1912, Canadian master John Scott sailed the *Success* to Boston after a stop-off in Cork, Ireland. The Irish in both cities felt a kinship with the *Success*'s former inmates and the money flowed in. The *Success* then worked the cities of the Eastern seaboard before heading south to pass through the new Panama Canal and make her way to the Panama-Pacific Exposition in San Francisco. It was there that she had a brush with glamour when, in 1915, Hollywood star Fatty Arbuckle came aboard for the filming of *Fatty and Mabel Visit the World's Fair*.

After a brief but profitable tour of the Pacific coast, the *Success* returned through the Panama Canal and sailed to the mouth of the Mississippi. In 1918, near Carrollton, Kentucky, she was caught in an ice gorge. When the gorge broke she began to move and damaged several other vessels before sinking. This was the beginning of *Success*'s decline. She was refloated and repaired, and toured the east coast for a few more years, but the crowds were becoming thin. In 1923, a period of economic depression, the *Success* was sold and her new owners took her on a tour of the Great Lakes.

The owners of the ship had no qualms about adding a little to the ship's history and its inventory of torture devices. They combed the castles and junk shops of England looking for instruments of pain, and even devised a few new ones of their own—nasty stretching machines mostly. A full-scale medieval rack was installed on the deck. A few extra whipping posts filled in some vacant corners below the main mast. And then there were the souvenirs. The ship was sheathed in copper and, apparently, the copper existed in an unlimited supply. Somewhere in England, a factory turned out cases of copper souvenirs, all of them stamped with an image of the *Success* under sail, and the statement "Original copper from the Convict Ship *Success*." Pieces of the copper sheeting of the *Success* were made into match cases, napkins rings, jewelry boxes, watch fobs, snuff boxes, spoons, and hearts. True, the ship had been overhauled and its hull re-sheeted in 1912, but so many of these souvenirs were made that even today they're not scarce. They can be picked up in flea markets or from online auctions for about $20 apiece, the same price, in relative terms, that visitors to the ship paid for them during the 1920s. Old handcuffs and other "original" fittings picked up in English junk shops were sold to more discerning yokels at premium prices.

To titillate the tourists, floggings and tortures were re-enacted on deck, using actors and—with some modifications—the gruesome machines. Postcards of "prisoners" receiving a (fatal) hundred lashes of the cat o' nine tails were sold on board, along with the other dubious merchandise. Below, wax dummies languished in cells and endured punishment from thumb screws (available to the very well-heeled collectors).

Still, there was enough of the original ship to horrify anyone who could see past the carnie show, including the little cells, more like stalls, that lined the walls of the musty hold of the ship, and the real punishment room, a tiny compartment in which the convict could neither stand nor sit comfortably. There was really no need for the rest of the contraptions. Anyone condemned to the *Success* had no secrets to divulge under torture. As in any other mid-nineteenth-century prison, the whip, the leather strap, the threat of starvation, and solitary confinement kept the toughest, most hardened men in line. Prisons built on land were hardly more comfortable than the prison ships in the nineteenth century. In both the United States and Canada small, unsanitary cells, solitary confinement, and the lash were by no means rare.

For five years, the *Success* drew huge crowds on both sides of the lakes and was always welcome in Chicago. She came back to the city as a main attraction of the 1933 Chicago Exposition before making a semi-permanent home in Cleveland.

But this was the 1930s: the Great Depression had settled in. Few people had money to spend on frivolous pastimes. Even fewer wanted to pay to see unhappy waxen people when there were so many real unhappy ones on the streets. The *Success*'s act had become old and tired. Just after the United States entered World War II, the ship was towed to Sandusky harbor, then to a mooring just outside Port Clinton, Ohio. There, her owner, Walter Kolbe, began stripping her of the valuable teak timbers and the old prison artifacts.

Most of the torture equipment ended up in homes in Ohio, and it's probably unfair to speculate on how much use its owners got from the racks, irons, and whipping posts. By the end of the 1930s, the ship was picked clean. She was still worth a fortune for the tons of teak and other exotic wood in her thick beams and hull. But no one got the chance to use that wood for furniture or for finishing better boats, even though, during World War II, that wood could have been put to good use by the navy. Looters cut the head off the *Success*'s figurehead in 1945. Then, on the afternoon of the Fourth of July, 1946, the *Success* went up in flames. The fire was almost certainly arson, but the culprits were never caught.

CHAPTER THIRTEEN

Death
Merchant

M ORE THAN THREE DECADES AGO, when I was growing up in the Georgian Bay shipbuilding town of Collingwood, I would sometimes meet my distant cousins who were orphans of the *Sand Merchant*. I knew then that at least one of those cousins' fathers had been blamed, to a greater or lesser degree, for the deaths of many of the *Sand Merchant*'s crew. Four of my grandfather's first cousins, and the husband of another cousin, died when the ship sank.

Dwight Boyer, dean of the Great Lakes shipwreck writers, wrote a chapter about the *Sand Merchant* in his book *Ships and Men of the Great Lakes*, which was published in 1977 to commemorate the loss of the *Edmund Fitzgerald*. I have avoided the subject. I did not include it in my first anthology of Canadian Great Lakes shipwreck stories published in 1995. I felt justified in leaving it out because the

The Sand Merchant *went about her business with little regard for the safety of her crew.*

book focused on Canadian tales and the *Sand Merchant* foundered in U.S. waters. Ten years later, when I wrote another book of shipwreck and disaster stories, this time from both sides of the lakes, I decided again to leave these family ghosts alone.

But one day in spring 2004, when I was waiting for a file to be delivered to me at the National Archives in Ottawa, I plugged the name *Sand Merchant* into the electronic catalogue. I expected, at most, maybe some correspondence, but the catalogue showed there were two thick files on the shipwreck, including a full report on its loss. I placed an order. The next day, it arrived from storage at the archive's cavernous new warehouse in Gatineau, Quebec.

I opened the box. The files, yellow and falling apart, were

stamped "Dormant." They had been declassified in 1995. They told the story that follows.

The *Sand Merchant* was built at the Collingwood shipyards in 1927. The ship, about half the size of a regular Great Lakes freighter, carried sand and gravel from shoals in the lakes to cement factories on both the Canadian and U.S. side of the lakes.

The *Sand Merchant* used giant vacuum pumps to suck its cargo from the lake bottom and dump it into the hold. Excess water drained back into the lake through screens. Several huge, supposedly water-tight, buoyancy tanks were built into the ship to keep it afloat in the worst weather. It was wet, cold, and poorly paid work for the crew, and it lacked the cachet of jobs aboard the big lake freighters. But, in the mid-1930s, in the depths of the Great Depression, work of any description was difficult to come by.

Most of the crew were men in their twenties and had landed jobs on the ship through personal or family connections. Wilfred Bourrie, the second mate, had found a place for his brother Danny in the crew. Wilfred also found work for three cousins, Hermann, Joseph, and Armas Dault, and his brother-in-law, Paul Robitaille. The six relatives were all from the little Georgian Bay lumbering village of Victoria Harbour or the nearby town of Midland.

Wilfred and Danny Bourrie's father, Ildege, was a carpenter who had built the interior of the Martyrs' Shrine on the edge of Midland and many of the houses and schools in the town. But there were precious few jobs like that to be had in the Dirty Thirties. Midland was in receivership and two-thirds of the population was out of work. The younger Bourries were in no position to be choosy. So, instead of following in their father's footsteps, Wilfred and Danny copied their older brother Francis in taking jobs on Great Lakes boats. Francis had earned his captain's papers and held a good job as an officer on a lake freighter of the Canada Steamship Lines.

New Brunswick-born Captain Graham McLelland, a beefy, middle-aged man, skippered the *Sand Merchant* in her last year. He had worked on the lake boats for twenty years but had never been given command of a full-sized freighter. The first mate, Bernard Drinkwalter, a man in his early forties, seems to have been a competent officer, but on the *Sand Merchant's* last trip he broke company rules, and a longstanding Great Lakes sailors' taboo, by bringing his wife Lillian along for the ride.

The *Sand Merchant* spent the summer of 1936 sucking gravel and sand from the bottom of Lake Ontario and taking it to Toronto. After a run from Toronto to Montreal, she sailed to Windsor, Ontario. On October 16, with a crew of twenty and Lillian Drinkwalter tucked away on board, the *Sand Merchant* set out for the sandbar that extends from the tip of Point Pelée, the southernmost part of mainland Canada. The ship arrived at 3:00 A.M. on October 17 and began filling her cargo hold. Water screened from the sand poured across her decks. The roar of her giant centrifugal sand pumps, and the lesser racket from the machinery in the ship's hold, added to the noise.

The captain dozed in his cabin through the morning of October 18. At 1:15 P.M., he came to the bridge and ordered the crew to hoist anchor and set out for Cleveland, fifty miles away. At her speed of seven to nine knots, she was expected to arrive at the narrow and treacherous entry to Cleveland's harbor in four-and-a-half hours, about dusk.

The wind was blowing about fifty miles an hour. Most ship captains on Lake Erie that day maneuvered for the protection of the north shore, but Captain McLelland had not taken a weather report because his ship had no radio. The barometer on the bridge was broken; it showed, all through the summer, a reading of 27 inches—hurricane level. The ship didn't even have a working compass. The captain kept a steady course across Lake Erie, relying on instinct to tell him his location and warn him of dangerous weather.

Near the middle of the lake, as the waves grew to about nine or ten feet, the cable to the steering gear broke. The captain ordered the ship to anchor, sailors restrung the cable, and, at about 6:00 P.M., the *Sand Merchant* resumed her trip. The captain went back to his cabin and left the ship in the hands of the second officer, Wilfred Bourrie.

At 8:30 on that pitch-black night, the *Sand Merchant* was about ten miles off the Ohio shore of Lake Erie, trying to find the narrow entrance to Cleveland harbor. The lack of a compass didn't help. Wilfred noticed the ship was developing a list to port of about five degrees. He called the captain's cabin.

From that time on, the first mate, who had supervised the loading, retreated into his cabin with his wife.

Captain McLelland went to the rear of the ship to inspect the cargo bins and found they'd taken a lot of water, turning the sand into a wet, heaving mass. Then he went to the bridge and ordered the ship's bow to be turned into the wind—away from Cleveland—to try to correct the list. This maneuver didn't work. In fact, the tilt of the ship increased and the waves, now driven by near gale-force winds blowing across the lake, became larger, and flowed across the *Sand Merchant's* decks.

Sometime after 9:30, the captain realized he was in serious trouble. He ordered the starboard anchor dropped, sent crew members to the deck to fire off flares and distress signals, and told Wilfred Bourrie, the only ship's officer he could find, to get out the lifeboats. The captain stayed on the bridge, working the engine controls and the ship's wheel. All of the ship's pumps were turned on, but the list increased.

While the crew scrambled on deck to light distress flares, set mattresses and bedding on fire to attract attention, and try to find the source of the leak, the captain did none of the things a ship's master was supposed to do when his vessel was foundering.

There were enough lifeboats on the *Sand Merchant* for her crew but, because the men had never had a boat drill, and because of the tilt of the ship, they couldn't launch the starboard boat. Instead, they cut its ropes and left it on the ship's deck to float away if the *Sand Merchant* sank.

The port boat was lowered into the water, but the crew stayed on the ship, hoping that someone would see the fires and flares on the deck. (A U.S. Coast Guard investigation later found people on the Ohio shore saw the flares and burning mattresses, but did nothing. No one called the police.) McLelland tried to find the Ohio shore to run the ship aground, but he was too late: the *Sand Merchant's* time was up.

At about 10:00 P.M., with just a few crew members in one lifeboat, the *Sand Merchant* took a sudden lurch, rolled over on her side, and sank in about sixty feet of water. The wave from the *Sand Merchant*'s death-plunge capsized both lifeboats. As his ship rolled over, the captain leaped from the bridge into the water.

The sailors who didn't go to the bottom with the ship surfaced to find themselves in the dark with two overturned lifeboats. There were nine hours of darkness ahead of them—nine hours before there was any chance of being seen by a passing ship.

A few moments after the ship went under, the men holding onto the two overturned lifeboats pushed them through the waves and linked them together. Wilfred Bourrie began a roll call. Fifteen people, including the Drinkwalters, drowned when the *Sand Merchant* sank. Eleven men—the captain, Second Mate Wilfred Bourrie, and sailors Daniel Bourrie, John Iderson, Ray Harper, Armas Dault, Hermann Dault, Martin White, John Meuse, William Clifford, and Frank Burns—survived the sinking and were struggling to stay alive in Lake Erie.

All through the night, Captain McLelland could see the lights of houses along the Ohio shore. Several ships passed within two or three miles of the drifting lifeboats. The *Sand Merchant*'s survivors had no flares to signal for help. "Later, I fell off the lifeboat and Dault pulled me up," the captain said the day after he lost his ship. He continued:

It wasn't bad until it got real cold this morning. The four others dropped off one by one. They seemed to go to sleep. They were too weak to say anything when they fell. The water was washing over the lifeboat so bad they couldn't say anything. It got worse after daylight.

I wouldn't have lasted much longer. And Iderson wouldn't have lasted ten minutes.

Hermann Dault spent the night trying to hang on to the keel of an overturned lifeboat and keep a grip on his younger brother, Armas. At least ten times that night, the waves pried him loose, and the two brothers had to climb up the side of the overturned boat.

> I was on the side the waves kept hitting all the time [he said later]. I was lying full length, with one hand on the keel and one hand hanging in the water, and the waves kept coming over us, and every time they would do that, we would have to bring our heads up for a gasp of breath, and that was during the first hour. I was told that Frank Burns was gone in the first hour.
>
> During the first hour Wilfred Bourrie kept saying, "Are you alright Danny?" and Danny kept answering and saying that he was alright. In the next half hour, there was no answer from Danny, and we found out that he had died and floated away. He had died with his grip on the keel.
>
> It seemed as if Wilfred had lost all his courage, and within the next hour Wilfred had slipped away."

By 3:00 A.M., the waves died down and the six remaining survivors no longer were in danger of being washed from the lifeboat. Just as the wind subsided, however, sailor Ray Harper died and floated away. The calm lasted about four hours and when the wind picked up again, "my brother went," said Hermann Dault.

> I couldn't hold him up any longer. I held onto him for
> four hours as it was. I kept slapping him to keep the
> blood circulating but I couldn't hold on. I was all
> exhausted. He didn't say anything when he went down.
> He just slipped.

Just before dawn, the two lifeboats became separated. William Clifford, clinging to one of the lifeboats with Martin White, who was dying of hypothermia, held tight as it drifted within three kilometers of the Ohio shore. And then a south wind pushed it back toward the center of the lake.

The first ship to come across the survivors was the freighter *Thunder Bay Quarries*. A few minutes later, the railway car ferry *Marquette & Bessemer No. 2* came across Clifford and White's upended lifeboat. White was too frozen to move, so sailors on the *Marquette & Bessemer No. 2* made a sort of sling to pull him aboard.

Later that day, J.L. Wodehouse, assistant steward on the *Thunder Bay Quarries*, told reporters in Sandusky, Ohio, the *Sand Merchant* survivors were in bad physical and emotional condition:

> [Hermann] Dault feels very bad. His brother dropped off
> the lifeboat thirty minutes before we rescued the three.
> As far as he knows, he lost two brothers. Dault was
> hanging on with just his nose out of the water, but the
> first thing he said to us is "Are the boys safe?" Iderson
> didn't even have a shoe on, just dungarees and a shirt.

The survivors were taken to Sandusky, Ohio, where some of them spent a few days in the hospital. By the end of the month, most of them were back at their homes. Subpoenas were delivered to them in the days that followed.

The widows and orphans of the *Sand Merchant's* crew got a form letter saying the Governor-General was saddened by their loss.

The inquiry into the loss of the *Sand Merchant* worked with a speed that can scarcely be imagined today. It began on November 12, 1936, just twenty-seven days after the *Sand Merchant* sank. It heard testimony for three days at the King Edward Hotel in Toronto. Its report was delivered to the government twelve days later.

Mr. Justice Errol McDougall of the Superior Court of Quebec headed the inquiry. He was unable to decide what caused the *Sand Merchant* to sink, but recommended technical studies to determine if there was a need to make changes to the design of that kind of vessel. Perhaps, he observed, water had somehow got into the ship's cargo of sand and caused it to become fluid enough to shift in the waves.

He did, however, know what did *not* cause the wreck of the *Sand Merchant*. No living person was to blame. No one with a lawyer at the hearing was found to have any liability.

James Clark, a member of the Ontario legislature, and Toronto lawyer P.N. Clark, were counsel for the commission. Three lawyers, John Jennings, R.D. Jennings, and S.L. Leckie represented the owners of the vessel, National Sand & Material Company Ltd. Lucien Beauregard was the lawyer for the insurers, and F.L.S. Jones represented the captain.

The families of the crew members had no counsel or standing in the hearing, but Wilfred and Danny Bourrie's brother Francis, a licenced Great Lakes captain, watched the proceedings and took notes:

> The loss of life must be laid at the charge of the First, and of the lesser degree of the Second, Officers of the said vessel, who were over-confident of the stability of the ship, and were not sufficiently alert in obeying the Master's orders to get the life-boats out and the crew aboard.
>
> The Court exonerates the Master from blame in the circumstances, but considers that he should be warned and is open to censure for failing to have life-boat drill aboard his vessel, and in permitting an unauthorized person to be aboard. The Operators of the vessel are held to be without blame for the occurrence, he [the inquiry] said.

Could the company or captain be blamed for the *Sand Merchant* heading into the darkness with neither barometer nor compass? No, the judge decided, because it wasn't against the law to rely on instinct to gauge weather conditions. Nor was it illegal to sail through pitch darkness with no functioning navigation equipment.

"No regulation requires that a ship shall be equipped with barometers, and their absence or inefficiency can scarcely be held to constitute negligence," he ruled. "A skilled seaman may rely on his experience as a proper indication of weather. That he obtained no weather forecast is not surprising, since his vessel was not equipped with wireless, nor did it require to be..."

Having the first mate's wife aboard, however, was judged by the inquiry to constitute a more serious lapse:

> From a somewhat different angle, the Master cannot be absolved from blame. He permitted the first officer to bring his wife aboard for the trip to Cleveland. No authority was obtained from the owners for such action and the purely customary privilege which is spoke on by the Master in such circumstances is no justification. In the sequel, this disregard of a rule, which is perhaps more honoured in the breach, may have contributed, and, in the opinion of the court, did contribute materially to the appalling loss of life which occurred.
>
> Distracted by the presence of his wife aboard, the first officer, who is shewn to have been a competent seaman, in the face of peril to all aboard, appears to have been solicitous as to his wife than to his obvious and paramount duty of getting the boats out and the crew aboard, as he had been directed by the Master.

Liability lay with two dead men, Drinkwalter and Wilfred Bourrie, the inquiry found. Both, of course, were beyond the reach of the law because they were dead.

> The responsibility for the loss of life which occurred must be laid on the shoulders of the First officer—and to a lesser degree on the second officer—first for failing to call the Master sooner, and second because he failed to

get the crew off the boat. Unfortunately, neither of these officers were present to explain their conduct, and became the victims of what must be regarded as their own failure to appreciate what was necessary in the emergency that faced them.

Few people who followed the case agreed with this verdict. The *Sand Merchant*'s file holds correspondence from sailors who believed McDougall was covering up for the captain and the ship's owners.

J. Leo Flynn of Oswego, New York, wrote to R.K. Smith, deputy minister of marine, challenging the verdict:

> Any captain who would put such a boat in the lake Saturday in view of the storm warnings and unusual barometric readings is not capable of his trust or is being pushed by his superiors. The latter is the biggest cause of loss of lives in marine circles today and should be curbed.
>
> Every boat at this port Saturday layed in on account of approaching storms and were in good judgment in so doing.

Just two days after the release of McDougall's report, Francis Bourrie wrote to the Minister of Justice, asking how a ship that was declared safe could be at the bottom of Lake Erie and its captain, who sailed the lakes on instinct alone, be found blameless.

> It appears to me had this [un-seaworthiness] been proven, the company would have had to go to the expense of making their ships seaworthy. In regards to

the steering apparatus, are you aware of the fact that there is an emergency steering gear on the boat deck of every vessel, with a compass, just for such occasions."

The captain also stated that his barometers were out of order and he notified the company. They didn't have them fixed. Why shouldn't they share their part of the responsibility?

His brother, Wilfred, had taken charge on deck and had tried to supervise the confused and untrained crew's launching of the lifeboats, only to be tagged with part of the blame for the deaths that occurred. Francis went on to argue the case for Wilfred:

At one time during the inquiry, Mr. Justice Errol McDougal remarked "was there only one man aboard that ship, it appears, the second mate was the only one in command." At another time, Major Clark, representing the Crown, remarked "it appears the second mate was the only one giving orders. It appears he was the only one in command."

When the Second Mate was ordered to get the lifeboats ready, did he not do his duty, when he got one lifeboat ready and found that he was the only officer in charge to try and get the other one ready. He had no orders to launch them. Besides, he had to put off the distress signals.

Was it the fault of the mates that the proper (whistle) signals to stand by the lifeboats, to lower lifeboats, to abandon ship, were not blown? Whose fault really was it then if it was left all to the second mate? From the evidence gathered from the survivors, my brother Wilfred John Bourrie fought to the last to save the crew. Even after he was in the water he done his duty by making the roll-call. What more could be asked of a man? If the ship was not seaworthy and his superior officers lacked in their duty in having boat drill, why should he be blamed when he is not here to defend himself?

Francis's letter was forwarded by the Minister of Justice to Minister of Marine C.D. Howe. Howe sent him a letter saying the government supported the inquiry's findings, but would investigate the design of the ship. He did not keep that promise.

Francis Bourrie shot back another letter to Howe blaming the ship's operators and demanding justice for his brother:

My brother, when speaking to me, always termed sand-suckers as death traps but with work so scarce he had no choice. The real fault of the loss of lives is that there are no laws to prohibit such death traps from operating.

The families of the dead crew members received nothing from either the ship's owners or the government.

Because the *Sand Merchant* sank in U.S. waters, its crew was not eligible for Ontario Workmen's Compensation. The widows of the sailors would have to find new husbands or jobs. Some of their children, among them the son of Wilfred Bourrie, were farmed out to relatives. Francis Bourrie adopted his nephew—Wilfred's son—Bev and raised him as his own son. Francis quit sailing, found a job as a Customs inspector, and was later a member of the village councils of Port MacNicoll and Victoria Harbour. After he died in 1993 Victoria Harbour named a street after him.

I felt strongly, as I read his letters, that it was time to clear Danny and Wilf's names.

One of the more poignant letters in the *Sand Merchant* file was sent by an elderly rural New Brunswick man, Hugh McInnis, to John Barry, the Member of Parliament for Northumberland County, New Brunswick. He hoped Barry would pressure the government into giving some financial help to the dependants of the dead sailors.

> I understand the question of a settlement with the dependents [*sic*] or between the company and dependents [*sic*] of those members of the crew of the S.S. *Sand Merchant* who lost their lives when the vessel sank in Lake Erie Oct. last is to be discussed in the House. If so please use your influence on my behalf, as my son Walter, one of the victims of the tragedy, was my only support and any financial aid would be a godsend.

Friends of McInnis also wrote to members of Parliament on his behalf, but lawyers for the ship owners pressured McInnis and the government into letting the issue die. In the end, only the *Sand Merchant*'s owners received compensation.

In early December, as McInnis pleaded with his representative for help, John Jennings, senior partner in the downtown Toronto law firm of Jennings and Clute, wrote to P.M. Anderson, the federal deputy minister of Justice:

My clients request that the Department will pay their solicitors' costs in connection with the preparation for, and their counsel fee for, appearing on the inquiry into the sinking of the "*Sand Merchant.*" It seems to them that this was an inquiry conducted in the public interest, and that the assistance my clients sought to render to the Commission and Commission counsel, was not a matter of their own interest at all, but in the public interest, and therefore should be paid out of public funds.

I shall be glad to hear from you if the department accept this view, and will pay the expenses to which my client company was put."

His invoice was paid.

CHAPTER FOURTEEN

Survivors

Rogers City, Michigan, is one of those quiet resort towns that line the Great Lakes. Pleasure boats fill the harbor in the summer, but Rogers City's docks were built for work, not play. Not far from the town docks, the home of Carl D. Bradley is a reminder of those times when small town entrepreneurs tried to build their towns into a new Chicago. Bradley was a visionary who, long before the building of the St. Lawrence Seaway, believed the lakes would become the great inland highway of North America. He built the Bradley Transportation Company into one of the great steamship firms on the lakes. In 1927, Bradley invested much of the company's capital in the construction of the largest self-unloading freighter on the Great Lakes.

In the Roaring Twenties, it wasn't considered immodest for a company president to name a ship after himself. Now, years after he has been forgotten, the name Carl D. Bradley still has a place in Great Lakes history, but for a reason that would have horrified the man himself.

The *Carl D. Bradley* carried limestone and coal to the steel mills along the lakes—not the most glamorous of careers. Still, in her early years, she was the biggest ship of her class, large enough to set cargo records that remained unbroken for years. She was a source of pride for the people of Rogers City whose population of around 3,000 provided almost every member of her crew.

The *Bradley* left a steel-mill pier at Gary, Indiana on November 18, 1958, and headed north. Her course was designed to take her up the length of Lake Michigan and on to Rogers City, on the shores of Lake Huron, where she was to be laid up for the winter. She was skippered by Captain Roland Bryan from Collingwood, Ontario, one of only three crewmen who weren't from Rogers City.

A powerful low-pressure system that had formed over the Pacific was, by the early hours of that day, centered over Lake of the Woods. It was slowed in its eastward progress by high-pressure systems over the Gulf of St. Lawrence and off Charleston, North Carolina. As the storm pushed up against the wall of cold air over Quebec it intensified. Its winds began as powerful, southwest-shifting gales at the front of the low. In its lee, storm-force winds from the north carried frigid Arctic air and snow whipped up from the open waters of the lakes.

Grand Marais, Minnesota, on the western shore of Lake Superior, was the first Great Lakes community to be hit by the storm. The winds swept away most of the town's commercial fishing fleet and destroyed the pleasure boats in the marinas. Seventy-five-mile-an-hour gusts pushed water into Grand Marais's main street and cut off Highway 61, the road out of town. Farther north, hurricane-force winds hit Port Arthur and Fort William, Ontario, tearing up trees, knocking down small buildings, forcing the closure of the ports, and stranding fifteen ships that were scheduled to leave on their last run of the season.

The *Bradley* was without a cargo, carrying only water ballast. As she headed almost due north, the gray waters of the lake began to kick up. Over the course of that November afternoon, the wind grew in strength from a sharp breeze to storm intensity. Twenty-foot waves crashed against the sides of the ship. The temperature dropped from just above freezing to twenty degrees Fahrenheit and ice started forming on the ship's handrail and wires.

On Georgian Bay, the *Eastern Shell*, a tanker out of Little Current, Manitoulin Island, barely limped into Owen Sound after four hours of mauling by sixty-mile-an-hour winds and twenty-five-foot waves. The captain, S.G. Williamson of Toronto, the third mate, George Beattie of Gaspé, Quebec, and wheelsman Aubrey Holden of Collingwood were in the pilothouse when a huge wave smashed through the main plate glass window. Flying glass severed tendons in the captain's right hand, sliced into his forehead, and cut his leg.

Three hours later, at Owen Sound, sailors carried Williamson down the gangplank to shore as the last winds of the storm pawed their ship. An ambulance took him to the local hospital. The other two men who had been on the bridge needed stitches to close their cuts but, unlike the captain, who needed surgery and a week in hospital, the officers were sent to a hotel overnight. Captain Williamson would leave Owen Sound scarred both by the glass shards and by a dreadful memory: Just an hour before Williamson was struck down on his own bridge, he heard a broadcast from his colleague on the *Carl D. Bradley*: "Take your life belts. This is it."

Just before 5:30 P.M., an amateur radio operator picked up the *Bradley's* first SOS. At 5:38, Coast Guard radio operator Roy Brunette picked up a message from Captain Bryan: "We've broken in half, we're going down." In Charlevoix, Michigan, a radio operator on duty that day remembered their call: "Mayday! Mayday! Mayday!... We are in serious trouble!... The ship is breaking up!" The *Eastern Shell* was one of dozens of ships that picked up a distress call from the *Bradley* and was too far away to be of any help.

All of the distress calls had been made by the forty-three-year-old first mate, Elmer Fleming. He was working in the pilothouse at 5:30, just before sunset, when he heard a loud thud. "Then we heard the alarm bells and looked around and saw the stern sagging," he reported later. "I didn't actually see the boat splitting in two. I spun around and looked back aft down the deck. I saw the stern of the boat was sagging and knew we were in trouble." He sent at least three distress calls and then went on deck. The ship rolled in the huge swells, tossing him over the waist-high railings and into Lake Michigan, some ten feet below. He continued the tale:

> It's strange and funny. I was in the pilothouse when the trouble started. When I finished my distress call I had no lifejacket. The line broke between fore and aft and I went out to pick up a jacket.

I managed to get through to the Coast Guard all around the Great Lakes, I learned later. When I came back up we were awash. The heavy superstructure started to turn the ship sideways. When we started to turn, she really went. I was thrown into the water and the raft came behind me.

Watchman Frank Mays, who was twenty-six at the time, landed in the water nearby. "I started my watch at four o'clock. I went up to the pilothouse and checked with the guys up there to see if they needed anything," Fleming told a meeting of history buffs at a conference at the Great Lakes Shipwreck Museum in Paradise, Michigan, in 1999.

Then, I went aft along the deck and the sea was getting up. I saw the men in the galley, and then went down to the engine room. I made my way forward in the tunnel, and I could see the old ship working—moving right before my eyes. I went up into the dunnage room, and that's where I heard a BANG—loudest noise I ever heard.

I looked aft along the port side and saw the stern of the *Bradley* swinging up and down just as your hand swings on your wrist at the end of your arm, and then went and got my lifejacket from my cabin.

The ship was going down quickly. I went up to the port side to see if that would be a good place to jump off, and it sure as heck wasn't. Then I went over to the starboard side, where the jumping wasn't any better—but at that moment the bow went over and threw me into the lake. I had my lifejacket on, but I sank pretty deep anyway. When my right hand reached out of the water, it immediately caught the edge of the life raft, and I climbed aboard as fast as I could.

Miraculously, he surfaced close to Fleming in the near-freezing water alongside the ship's pontoon raft. Within a few minutes, two other sailors managed to climb aboard. In the twilight, they could see the broken *Bradley* being tossed by thirty-foot waves, rollers as big as two-storey houses. The bow end of the ship settled into the water and slipped under. The stern, her cabins still lit by the ship's power generators, stayed up a little longer. In the ship's lights, Fleming and the three other men aboard the raft could see sailors trying to escape the doomed stern. None of them made it. The *Carl D. Bradley*'s two lifeboats were empty when the ship sank 300 feet to the bottom of Lake Michigan.

"We looked back at the ship and saw the stern go straight down," Fleming said. "There was an explosion when the last part of the stern went under."

The distress call gave Fleming and the three other survivors a fighting chance. Two hours after the call went out, the German steamship *Christian Sartori,* which had been just a few miles from the *Bradley* when she sank, reported spotting wreckage: a large fuel tank and a raincoat. "I believe all hands are lost," the captain of the *Sartori* reported to radio operator Brunette at Port Washington. The German captain told Brunette he heard a fierce explosion at about 5:30 in the afternoon. The *Sartori* began firing off flares to draw rescuers to the scene.

An hour after the sinking, officials of the company that owned the *Bradley* drove to the homes of crewmen in Rogers

City and told their families that the ship was lost. They stayed up listening to their radios for the rest of the night. The news was grim: the *Bradley* sank in a fairly isolated part of the lake, southwest of Beaver Island, about halfway between the Michigan and Wisconsin shores. She foundered near Gull Island, the same small rock where, in the Great Storm of 1913, the crew of the *L.C. Waldo* fought for their lives. The storm abated in the night, but no survivors were picked up.

While the families of the *Bradley's* crew spent that terrible night hoping for a miracle, a terrible drama was unfolding on the pontoon raft.

"I knew a couple [of men] were there," Fleming later said, describing how two others joined him and Frank Mays aboard the raft. "I heard some fellows hollering. There were a lot of ring preservers with lights which lit up the area. Frank and I called in to two other fellows who swam over to our raft.

"But we lost them during the night. We lost the first man about 11:30 P.M. when the waves tossed the raft into a complete flip. We were all thrown into the water. I gurgled and bubbled and swam until I came across the raft and then, somehow, I managed to get back on it. Then I helped the others. That's how it was all three times that it flipped."

Despite the horror of that long night in Lake Michigan's frigid water, Mays never doubted they'd be rescued. "But I never stopped praying," he told newspaper reporters the day after the disaster.

Fleming and Frank Mays clung to the wooden life raft for fourteen-and-a-half hours. At dawn, they were spotted by the crew of the Coast Guard cutter *Sundew*, which had, at no small risk to her crew, spent the night fighting the storm and following up on the leads given to it by the *Sartori*. The two men, the only survivors of the worst Lake Michigan disaster since the Armistice Day Storm of 1940, were found between Gull and High Islands, several miles from the *Bradley's* location given in Fleming's last report.

The *Sundew* spotted the raft about 7:00 A.M. and picked the two survivors from the lake. Both men wanted the *Sundew* to keep searching the area rather than head for port. When the cutter finally did arrive at Charlevoix, Michigan on the evening of the nineteenth, it carried eight corpses of Mays and Fleming's crewmates.

The day after Mays and Fleming were rescued, reporters were allowed into their hospital room to photograph them with their wives. Marlys Mays said, "I'm happy, but I'm sorry so many other wives are so sad. Frank will be twenty-seven on Monday. We're going to have a big Thanksgiving, Christmas, and birthday party all rolled into one."

But there were far less happy stories to be found in Rogers City, which had lost thirty-one of its men on the *Bradley*. Caroline Krawczak, the wife of sailor Joseph Krawczak, opened her home to reporters and allowed them to photograph her six children, ranging in age between eighteen months and eleven years old.

Within three days, the Coast Guard and 150 police and civilian volunteers who walked the shores of the islands near the wreck site found eighteen bodies. A second Coast Guard cutter joined the *Sundew*, and three helicopters and two airplanes flew grid patterns over the 750-square mile wreck area as hope faded for more survivors. Life jackets littered the shores and an empty lifeboat washed up on High Island.

"Weather conditions are against us," Chief Warrant Officer Joseph Etienne, commander of the Charlevoix coast guard region, said to reporters two days after the sinking. "But the service always feels there is a possibility that a man might be found alive."

It was a faint hope. One Rogers City doctor said the survival of Mays and Fleming was "an amazing piece of human endurance." He said there was little hope for other survivors, "even if they made it to land."

Saturday, November 22 was declared a day of mourning in Rogers City by Mayor Kenneth P. Vogelheim. One resident told a newspaper reporter: "It's like one of those mine disasters we read about. They went out Monday morning and they won't be back. All we can do is wait."

But there was nothing to wait for. Fleming and Mays were the only survivors. Fleming worked for the Bradley company for another nineteen years. He died in the 1990s. Today, Mays is the last of the *Bradley*'s men alive. He is retired and lives safely on dry land in Florida. But in 1995, he took a submersible trip down to the wreck of the *Bradley*. He noticed the red paint he had applied to the handrails three days before the ship left Gary still looked fresh.

In the shipping season of 1966, Dennis Hale was still learning the ropes. He was the same age as Mays when the *Bradley* sank and had been sailing for just three years. The money was good, the work was hard but, as a young, single man, Hale didn't mind being away from home for most of

One storm too many for the Morrell *led to a dreadful tale of survival at sea.*

the year. He had worked on just one ship, the 580-foot freighter *Daniel J. Morrell.*

The *Morrell,* in its sixtieth year, was nearly three times older than Hale. It was one of the replacement ships built in the years after the Great Storm of 1913 cleared the Great Lakes of their best and newest vessels. After World War II, there was a surplus of shipping capacity and many of the older, smaller ships were scrapped. The *Morrell* was good enough to survive the culling, but she had definitely earned out her investment. Her sister ship, the *Edward J. Townsend,* was also ready to be cut up. Hale, however, was looking forward to a sailing career that should have lasted another forty years, one that would end in the early years of the twenty-first century. But on November 29, the nautical career of both man and ship would end in a pounding gale in northern Lake Huron.

Hale should have been paid off and at home that day. The *Morrell* had officially finished the 1966 season and was supposed to be laid up in a Michigan port. She stayed in service to make one last trip, called in when another ship's engine broke down. Because of the problems of that other ship, their owners, the Bethlehem Steel Company, sent the *Morrell* and the *Townsend* from Detroit to Taconite Harbor, Minnesota, where each would pick up a load of iron ore.

Captain Arthur Crawley had twenty-five years of experience on the lakes, but this was his first season as captain of the *Morrell*. On board the *Townsend*, Captain John Connelly kept his ship a few miles back of the *Morrell* as they headed up the lake. The winds sent waves broadside across the decks of the ships. Both captains struggled to keep their ships' bows into the wind as the waves grew from ten feet to twenty. As they sailed through the south Lake Huron waters that had claimed so many sailors in the Great Storm of 1913, they considered turning back to the safety of the St. Clair River. Instead, they decided to continue north, and, if need be, take shelter in Thunder Bay, Michigan.

By midnight, snow squalls battered the two ships. They were barely making walking speed, moving through the walls of water at just three knots. They were without cargo, weighted with water ballast, and they twisted and turned in the wind and the currents. Both captains had seen storms before. So had their ships. Indeed, the *Morrell* had fought the same Lake Michigan storm that took the *Bradley*. But years of this kind of stress had taken its toll.

Sometime after midnight the *Morrell*'s hull was broken. The split spread through the plating about midway along the deck. Those who were awake through the storm and the break-up of the *Morrell* had just a few minutes to make the right moves.

Hale was asleep in his cabin in the bow at 2:00 A.M. when he heard a loud bang. The Morrell was off the coast of northern Michigan, rounding the "thumb" that separates the main part of the lake from Saginaw Bay. The first sign of trouble was the lights blinking. Hale thought there was some kind of problem with the generators. Then books tumbled from a shelf. That was normal in a heavy storm. Hale tried to convince himself the noise that woke him up was just the sound of the anchor thumping against the ship's hull, but when he heard a second, louder bang, he jumped out of bed, pushed his way down a short hallway, opened the cabin door and saw something he could not possibly forget. The *Morrell*'s deck twisted like a snake, mauled by sixty-five-mile-an-hour winds and twenty-five-foot waves. The awful sound that had awakened Hale was the ship's death rattle: she was coming apart. Even in the darkness, Hale could see the cracks ripping across the deck.

Hale was not dressed for this. He was wearing boxer shorts and a light jacket. He stood in his bare feet in the ice and water on the deck. Rather than turn back and get warmer clothes, he pulled himself along a deck rail, looking for one of the *Morrell*'s lifeboats or its single raft.

What was his most vivid memory of the wreck? "It was the noise around me," he said. "The wind through the wires, the steel crunching, steam escaping, the laboring of the engine. It was very prominent."

When he reached the life raft, several crewmen were already inside or standing nearby, waiting to get in. The power cables had been severed by the ship's breakup, and the bow was in the dark. The split happened so quickly that no SOS had been sent before the bridge lost power.

"I heard a noise behind me," Hale said. "The main deck was starting to tear. There were sparks, little puffs of smoke. I watched it [the ship] separate. I was looking over my shoulder, thinking 'God, I hate to get wet.' I wasn't in panic. I always thought that was quite strange."

Hale and the men on the bow of the *Morrell* were luckier than those at the stern. The sailors at the bow at least knew no SOS had been sent and there would be no quick rescue. The men on the stern, which was now pulling away from the rest of the ship, stayed on their well-lit and relatively dry end of the *Morrell* and fired off flares to attract the attention of rescuers. Winds approaching hurricane strength blew the flares sideways and doused them. No would-be rescuer saw them. Perhaps the crew on the stern thought their sister ship would come to their assistance. But the *Townsend* had lost track of the *Morrell*. She would survive the storm but not its aftermath: the *Townsend* was declared unfit for service in the weeks that followed and never made another voyage.

At the bow, the bridge crew and sailors waited in the life raft for the *Morrell* to go down. These thirteen men watched in horror as the *Morrell* took a couple of final twists and separated completely. The stern slammed into the bow section. Huge pieces of deck plating swiped at the men huddled on the raft. Finally, the stern, and the sixteen men on it, began drifting away. Within minutes, the bow sank. The raft tumbled into the lake, tossing all the sailors off. Somehow, blinded by darkness and caught in the coils of the huge, black waves, Hale surfaced close to the raft. Three other men—the captain and the first and second mates—also found it and, as Hale had done, climbed aboard. And then they watched as the stern of the *Morrell*, still lit, drifted off into the night. It sank about fifteen minutes later.

"I can still see the sparks and the tearing steel," Hale remarked quietly from his home in Ashtabula, Ohio.

> The next thing I knew, I was in the water. When I came to the surface, I saw a raft and swam over to it. By the time I got there, two other men had climbed aboard, and we then helped a fourth man on. It was freezing cold and snowing. All I could do was hang on. The storm was over by 5:00 A.M., but by then, two of the men were already dead. The other one died later on.

Throughout that long day no sign of rescue came in sight. "I didn't expect to make it. For the last twenty-four hours I was more or less just waiting to die. When you're in a situation like that you don't care. You just want it to end. It wasn't important anymore."

"I really don't know how to die," he said. "Life had always been a struggle for me. My mother died when I was young, and I was pretty much on my own since I was thirteen years old. I had the will to survive."

Maybe the three other men aboard the raft also had the will to survive. But hour after hour, all through that night, the following day, the next night, and the morning of November 30, the cold and wind sapped the life out of them. Three of the four men on the raft expired.

"They died within minutes of each other," Hale said later. "Their lungs filled with water." The lifeboats themselves must have been swamped at this point.

Hale wore fewer clothes than any of them, and later he credited this with his survival. The other men, he said, were covered with a glaze of ice that clung to their clothes. He was not so icily encumbered.

By the first morning after the wreck of the *Morrell*, the Coast Guard and the media knew the ship was missing. Although the storm had passed, Hale and his companions were not nearly as lucky as Fleming and Mays, who had been rescued relatively quickly. Despite the improvements in search-and-rescue technology in the eight years after the sinking of the *Bradley*, nearly a day-and-a-half passed before the Coast Guard found any wreckage or bodies from the *Morrell*. By then, Hale was huddled, just half alive, under the bodies of his captain and the two mates. The still-warm corpses made enough of a shelter to keep the half-naked Hale alive.

A Coast Guard helicopter spotted the life raft just south of Harbor Beach, Michigan. That afternoon's newspapers carried photos of a Coast Guard helicopter plucking Hale to safety. The chopper flew him to the hospital in Harbor Beach. Doctors found Hale had a body temperature of ninety-two degrees, had broken his ankle when he was tossed into the lake, and he had fairly mild frostbite on his fingers and toes.

At the Harbor Beach hospital, Hale asked to see a priest. "Father, why am I alive?" the twenty-six-year-old man asked Father Cornelius McEchin. "Because God wants you to be alive," the priest answered.

Over the years, that answer hasn't always sustained Hale. He quit sailing, and for years lived as a recluse. He found work as a tool-and-die maker, moving from job to job in Ohio and Kentucky. Four marriages failed. He went to priests, psychologists, even to a hypnotist, to try to come to grips with what happened on the *Morrell* and in the turbulent lake afterwards.

"It seems as though I was always on the run," he told a newspaper reporter thirty-five years after the disaster. "I think the post-traumatic stress syndrome had something to do with it. I was very unsettled, very frightened. I was trying to outrun something." Finally, he wrote a book, *Sole Survivor*, about his ordeal. Instead of hiding from the world and from the Great Lakes, he's now a frequent speaker at historical societies and marine museums. There are still aspects of the disaster he can't talk about, but he's finally doing well. In 1999, he took his first trip on the lakes since the sinking, a five-day sojourn as a passenger on the lake freighter *Roger Blough.*

"There's got to be some reason I survived. Maybe I'm supposed to give others hope. Maybe hearing my story inspires people. I talk at these shipwreck conferences." He has addressed eight such gatherings in the past year and has four more to go. "People are real interested. It puts a shift in their perspective."

Notes on Sources

Chapter One: Brawling on Lake Erie

The U.S. Brig Niagara reconstruction group's website, www.brig-niagara.org, has reprints of some of the primary source material from the battle. Its Canadian counterpart, the rebuilders of the HMS *Detroit*, has posted British material at www.hmsdetroit.org/battle.htm. See "Afterword to the Battle of Lake Erie," *Inland Seas*, 33:3 (1977): 180–83; "Battle of Lake Erie (a Roster with Notes)," *Inland Seas*, 4:4 (1948): 245–48; "Battle of Lake Erie after 175 years: Commemoration and Controversy," *Inland Seas*, 48:3 (1988) 264–73; "Battle of Lake Erie in the War of 1812," *Inland Seas*, 43:3 (1987): 178–87; "Brief Sketches of the Officers Who Were in the Battle of Lake Erie," *Inland Seas*, 19:3 (1963): 172–89; "British Personnel at Battle of Lake Erie," *Inland Seas*, 54:4 (1998): 298–314; "Other Hero of the Battle of Lake Erie," *Inland Seas*, 44:4 (1988): 274–80; "Racing Sailor Looks at the Battle of Lake Erie," *Inland Seas*, 44:2 (1988): 132–3. For a brief description of Perry and his colleagues, see

Peterson, Charles J., *The Military Heroes of the War of 1812* (Philadelphia: William A Leary & Co., 1849); Goldowsky, Seebert J., *Yankee Surgeon: The Life and Times of Usher Parsons, 1788–1868* (Boston: The Francis A. County Library of Medicine, in cooperation with the Rhode Island Publications Society, 1988); Malcolmson, Robert, *Sailors of 1812: Memoirs and Letters of Naval Officers on Lake Ontario During the War of 1812* (Annapolis: Naval Institute Press, 1990). The *Niagara*'s actions on the upper lakes after the battle are described in *Ontario Historical Society Papers and Record*, Vol. 9 (1910).

Chapter Two: The Witch of November

For a description of the fierce warfare in upstate New York, see Allen, Robert S., *His Majesty's Indian Allies: British Indian Policy in the Defence of Canada, 1774–1815* (Toronto: Dundurn Press, 1992). The best primary source information on the loss of the *Ontario* is found in the papers of General Frederick Haldimand held in the National Archives of Canada. For a description of the *Ontario*, see Dillon, Richard C., "Reconstruction of the *Ontario*," *Inland Seas*, 47:2 (1991): 96–98. Frank Barcus wrote the definitive account of the Great Storm of 1913. His book, *Freshwater Fury* (Detroit: Wayne State University Press, 1960), is out of print, but may be found in research libraries. The Great Storm is standard fare for Great Lakes shipwreck books. See works by Bowen, Boyer, and Ratigan. The best material on the storm can be found in newspapers of the time. The *Toronto Star, Toronto Globe*, and the *London Free Press* did excellent reporting on the disaster and stayed on the story through the inquests in the winter of 1913–14. For a description of the discovery of the *Charles S. Price*, see *Inland Seas*, 42:2 (1982), 11–15. The discovery of the wreck of the *Regina* is described in *Inland Seas*, 43:2. See also:

"*Leafield* was Unlucky," *Inland Seas*, 3:3 (1947): 143–44; "Mysterious Sinking of the *Charles S. Price*," *Inland Seas*, 42:2 (1986): 102–14; "Wreck of the *Wexford*," *Inland Seas*, 31:2 (1975): 154; "Great Storm of 1913 Remembered," *Inland Seas*, 44:3 (1988): 154–69; "Great Storm of November 9, 1913," *Inland Seas*, 2:2 (1946): 34–35. For a discussion of the Luddite attitude of some early twentieth-century Great Lakes captains, see "Reluctant Acceptance of Wireless Use on the Great Lakes," *Inland Seas*, 49:2 (1993): 149–53. For a discussion of the attitudes of some captains, see Bourrie, Mark, *True Canadian Stories of the Great Lakes* (Toronto: Prospero, 2004). The chapter on the loss of the steamer *Arlington* in 1940 relates inquiry testimony on captains' attitudes to barometers. The Armistice Day storm was given wide coverage. Along with the crews of the vessels lost on the Great lakes, some 200 duck hunters died in Minnesota during the storm. See O'Meara, T., "Big Blow," *Inland Seas* 2:4 (1946): 236–39; and a first-person account by Captain R.W. Parsons, "Storm of 1940," *Inland Seas*, 17:3 (1962): 202–06. Robert Hemming's *Gales of November* (Chicago: Contemporary Books, 1981) was written with the cooperation of family members of the *Fitzgerald*'s crew. It is the definitive work on the disaster. Frederick Stonehouse, *The Wreck of the Edmund Fitzgerald* (AuTrain, Michigan: Avery Color Studios, 1977), contains considerable material from the official inquiry into the *Fitzgerald* disaster. See also: Ratigan, William, *Great Lakes Shipwrecks and Survivals* (Grand Rapids, Michigan: Wm. B. Eerdsmans, 1977). The recovery of the *Fitzgerald*'s bell is described in "Bell of the *Fitzgerald*," *Inland Seas*, 51:3 (1995): 6–8.

Chapter Three: Remember the Caroline

"Last Battle of Lake Erie," *Inland Seas*, 13:3 (1957): 205–06. For a detailed account of the destruction of the *Caroline* and the Battle of the Windmill, see Lindsay, Charles, *The Life and Times of Wm. Lyon Mackenzie* (Toronto: P.R. Randall, 1862). See also Schull, Joseph, *Rebellion* (Toronto: Macmillan of Canada, 1971). The *Canadian Historical Review* has published several papers that are useful for the study of the *Caroline* incident and the subsequent military action. See Landon, R., "The Common Man in the Era of the Rebellion in Upper Canada," *CHR* (1937): 76; New, J., "The Rebellion of 1837 in Its Larger Setting, (Presidential Address)," *CHR* (1937): 5; Ouelette, P., "Papineau dans la révolution de 1837–1838," *JHC*, (1958): 13. For an interesting look at Bond Head and Mackenzie, see Wise, Sydney, *Sir Francis Bond Head: A Narrative* (Ottawa: Carleton University Press, 1969).

Chapter Four: The *Atlantic*

For an excellent website with pictures and a description of the litigation, see www.kwic.com/~pagodavista/atlantic.html. My own account of the litigation, in which I examined the judgement and interviewed counsel, appeared in the May 2000 issue of *Canadian Lawyer*. See also "Loss of the Steamer *Atlantic*" as told by Amos Girdwood, wheelsman, *Inland Seas*, 20:3 (1964): 211–14. A number of writers have taken sides over the issue of who was entitled to the money recovered from the *Atlantic*. For information about the salvaging effort, see *Buffalo News* (May 5, 1994): B6; *Financial Post* (May 6, 1994): 39; *Los Angeles Times* (June 6–7, 1994): Metro 1; *Los Angeles Times* (June 26, 1994): Metro 1; Mesa (Arizona) *Tribune* (August 2, 1992). I also referred to a press release, "Canadian Actions to Preserve Historic

Shipwreck Supported by New York State and Pennsylvania Officials," broadcast by Business Wire (BRW), July 16, 1991, available through the Associated Press archives.

Chapter Five: The Wreck of the *Lady Elgin*

Good primary source material for the loss of the *Lady Elgin* can be found in the Chicago and Milwaukee newspapers of the summer of 1860. The *London Illustrated News* carried a two-page article with engravings in its August 1860 issue. See Boyer, Dwight, *True Tales of the Great Lakes* (Cleveland: Freshwater Press, 1971). See also: "One Hundredth Anniversary of the *Lady Elgin*," *Inland Seas*, 16:1 (1960): 4–13; and "Slavery, Secession, and a Steamer," *Inland Seas*, 54:2 (1998). An excellent website with archaeological information and rare photos: www.shipwrecks.net/shipwreck/projects/.

Chapter Six: The *Michigan*

For a good account of James Strang and his strange times, see *Beaver Island Journal*, 1:1, 9–27. The Beaver Island Historical Society's web site, www.beaverisland.net/History, contains useful information, and the society holds a first-rate collection of Strang memorabilia that is open to the public at its museum in Jamestown. For more about the *Michigan*, see "U.S. Government Service on the Great Lakes," *Inland Seas*, 24:1 (1968): 59–60; "The 106-Year Career of a Beautiful Ship: The Story of the USS *Michigan*," *Inland Seas*, 50:1 (1994): 4–13; "Civil War and Great Lakes Steamers," *Inland Seas*, 15:4 (1959): 256–70; "Confederate Prisoners of War on Lake Erie," *Inland Seas*, 52:4 (1996): 302–10; "Confederate Raiders on Lake Erie," *Inland Seas*, 5:1

(1949): 42, and 5.2 (1949): 101–05. Mayer, Adam, *Dixie and the Dominion* (Toronto: Dundurn Press, 2003) is an excellent study of Confederate operations in Canada, including the *Philo Parsons* incident. The *Toronto Globe,* owned at the time by influential politician George Brown, covered the U.S. court cases that arose from the *Philo Parsons* incident and the other Lake Erie raids. In late 1864, stories appeared under the heading "Lake Erie Pirates." For more information on Denison and the *Georgian,* see Denison, George Jr., *The Petition of George Taylor Denison Jr. to the Honourable the House of Assembly Praying to Redress the Matter of the Seizure of the Steamer "Georgian,"* (Toronto: Leader and Patriot Steam Press Establishment, 1865). See also MacLean, Guy, "The *Georgian* Affair," *Canadian Historical Review*, 52: 2. Thompson's activities became public when the Union Republican Congressional Committee reprinted his reports in 1868, possibly to strengthen the hand of Radical Republicans in the congressional elections that year. A copy of the report is on file in Canada's National Library in Ottawa. The best book on Canadian–U.S. relations during the Civil War is Winks, Robin W., *Canada and the United States: the Civil War Years* (Baltimore: Johns Hopkins University Press, 1960). For more information about Bennett Burleigh and his fantastic generation of war correspondents, see Knightley, Phillip, *The First Casualty* (New York: Harcourt Brace Jovanovich, 1975). For information on the Fenian Raids, see the Queen's Own Rifles of Canada website, www.qor.com/history/ridgeway.html. The small museum on the Ridgeway battlefield was closed in 2004, but the museum in the nearby village of Ridgeway has an excellent collection of artifacts, brochures, and postcards of paintings made on the battlefield by an artist brought by the Fenians. See also "Green Flags and Red-Coated Gunboats: Naval Activities on the Great Lakes during the Fenian Scare," *Inland Seas*, 22:2 (1966): 91–110; "Gunboats on the Lower Lakes during the Fenian Scare, *Inland Seas*, 19: 1

(1963): 47–54. For a discussion of the *Michgian*'s later years, see "Explosion on the *USS Michigan*," *Inland Seas*, 16:1 (1960): 32–35; "Great Lakes Lady Bares Her Fangs," *Inland Seas*, 14:1 (1958): 58–60; and "Save the *Wolverine!*" *Inland Seas*, 1:1 (1945): 36–37.

Chapter Seven: Fire!

"Burning of the *Phoenix*," *Inland Seas*, 14:1 (1958): 26–35; "Shattered Dreams: The Burning of the *Phoenix*," *Inland Seas*, 30:3 (1974): 159–67. Sheboygan historian Bill Wangemann tells the story of the *Phoenix* at http://freepages.genealogy.rootsweb.com/~sheboygan/phoenix.htm. For information about the loss of the *E.K. Collins*, see the town of Goderich website, www.town.goderich.on.ca/marine/shipwrecks.htm, and J.B. Mansfield's www.linkstothepast.com/marine/chapt37.html. For information on the *Seabird*, see www.chicagosite.org/uasc/seabird.htm. For the *Clarion*, see "Heroes of the *Clarion*," *Inland Seas*, 54:4 (1998): 254–56. For a brief description of the *Noronic*, see *Inland Seas*, 5:1. For a longer description of sailing life on the *Noronic*, with a photograph of the ship, see "Magnificent *Noronic*," *Inland Seas*, 52:4 (1996): 42–49. The *Noronic* fire is mentioned in most Great Lakes shipwreck books. A chilling account of the fire is in *Perils of the Deep*, 1:1 (1994), a magazine published in Canoga Park, California, by Challenge Publications Ltd. It may be difficult to find. Quite explicit reportage of the fire was published in the *Toronto Star*, whose coverage by Ed Feeny was stellar. Mr. Feeny died in March, 1995. Jim Hunt's reporting on the fire in the *Toronto Telegram* was solid eyewitness work by a top journalist. Excellent coverage of the fire on the *Cartiercliffe Hall* was carried by the Associated Press.

Chapter Eight: Alexander McDougall's Whalebacks

See Feltner, C. & J., *Great Lakes Maritime History: A Bibliography and Sources of Information* (Dearborn: Sea Jay Publications, 1982); Lydecker, R., *Pigboat: The Story of the Whalebacks*, (Superior, Wisconsin: Head of the Lakes Maritime Society, 1981); and Ratigan, William, *Great Lakes Shipwrecks and Survivals* (New York: Galahad Books, 1974). See also "Bicycling on the *Christopher Columbus*," *Inland Seas*, 52:4 (1996): 264–65; "*Christopher Columbus*, a Favorite in Her Day," *Inland Seas*, 29:2 (1973): 128; "McDougall's White Swan—the First Voyages of the *Christopher Columbus*," *Inland Seas*, 49:3 (1993): 180–84. The city of Superior, Wisconsin, has established a museum devoted to the whalebacks and owns a website with valuable data: www.superiorpublicmuseums.org.

Chapter Nine: Four Mysteries

Dwight Boyer's *Ghost Ships of the Great Lakes* (New York: Dodd, Mead, 1968) gives a full account of the loss of the *Marquette & Bessemer No. 2*, which he wrote with the help of crew family members. His account carries a suggestion of foul play. See also Hepburn, Agnes M., *Historical Sketch of the Village of Port Stanley* (Port Stanley: Port Stanley Historical Society, 1952) and Hilton, George Woodman, *The Great Lakes Car Ferries* (Berkley: Howell-North, 1962). Initial newspaper accounts of the sinking of the ship and the retrieval of bodies were somewhat sparse. The best coverage of the sinking was in the Cleveland newspapers. Most material on the loss of the minesweepers comes from coverage in the *Thunder Bay Chronicle* and the *Toronto Globe*. For a description of the loss of the two minesweepers, see Wrigley, R., *Shipwrecked* (Cobalt, Ontario: Highway Book Store, 1985). See also Mauro, Joseph R., *A History of Thunder Bay*, (Thunder Bay, Ontario: City of Thunder Bay, 1981).

Chapter Ten: The Christmas Tree Ships

Chicago's hyper-competitive early twentieth-century press gave the loss of the *Rouse Simmons* "end of the world" front page play. See also "Christmas Tree Ship," *Inland Seas* 18:3 (1962): 240. There are several excellent websites devoted to the Chicago Christmas tree ships. See, for example, www.christmastreeship. homestead.com; the Coast Guard's Christmas tree ship program, www.boatsyachtsmarinas.com/history/html/xmas_tree_ship.html; www.gapersblock.com/airbags/archives/the_real_christmas_schooner/; and www.jsonline.com. Other sources: Associated Press, November 27, 2004; *Muskegon Chronicle*, November 28, 2004; and *Chicago Daily Herald*, February 4, 2005.

Chapter Eleven: Unsafe at Any Speed

For a disaster that, outside of Chicago, has slipped from public memory, there is a great deal of primary source material available. Every newspaper in North America covered the wreck. Reporters from the Chicago papers, which supplied most of those stories to the news services, interviewed hundreds of survivors. I relied primarily on the *Chicago Tribune* and stories carried in the *Toronto Globe* and the *Toronto Star*. Material on the loss of the *Eastland* can be found in "Just What Was the Cause of the *Eastland* Disaster?" *Inland Seas*, 15:3 (1959): 200–06; "Tragedy of the *Eastland*," *Inland Seas*, 16:3 (1960): 190–95; "*Eastland*—A Half-Century Ago," *Inland Seas*, 21:2 (1965): 115–21; "Chicago's Missing U-Boat," *Inland Seas*, 45:1 (1989): 2–9. The *Eastland*

Historical Society maintains one of the best shipwreck websites at www.eastlanddisaster.org.

Chapter Twelve: The Convict Ship *Success*

Material for this chapter comes from a booklet printed by the owners of the *Success* for its visit to the San Francisco World's Fair. See also "Convict Ship *Success*," *Inland Seas*, 2:4 (1946): 276; "Australia and the *Success*," Inland Seas, 3:2 (1947): 106–112. For an excellent website see www.home.gci.net/~alaskapi/success.

Chapter Thirteen: Death Merchant

Most of the material for this chapter came from the National Archives of Canada's file on the inquiry into the loss of the *Sand Merchant*. The National Archives holds the transcripts of the official inquiry, the correspondence of the principals involved, and the subsequent correspondence between Francis Bourrie and government officials. The *Toronto Star* of October 20, 1936 carried a story on the loss of the *Sand Merchant* and many pictures of her crew and captain.

Chapter Fourteen: Survivors

The *Globe and Mail* (Toronto) carried a wire service and staff report on the loss of the *Carl D. Bradley*, November 19, 1958, p. 1, that was written before the discovery of the survivors, as well as a National Weather Service map showing the size and track of the storm (p. 2). The following day's edition carried the Associated Press dispatch and photograph from Charlevoix,

Michigan, describing the rescue of Fleming and Mays, and a sidebar on the reaction of Rogers City to the tragedy. These stories were moved on the news wires and used throughout North America. The *Toronto Star*, then still an afternoon paper, carried other wire service pictures of the survivors and their families, and a photograph of the *Carl D. Bradley* in its November 19 edition (p. 2). For a photo and description of the *Carl D. Bradley* and her loss, see www.mhsd.org/publications/glswr/bradley/htm. For a description of a diving expedition to the *Carl D. Bradley*, see www.boatnerd.com/bradley. Historian Skip Gilham describes the *Bradley* at http://vos.noaa.gov/MWL/dec_04/Bradley.shtml. Marine historian James Donahue describes the rescue of Mays and Fleming at http://perdurabo10/tripod.com/id582.html. Dennis Hale has written a book (with Pat Stayer and Jim Stayer) about his incredible rescue on Lake Huron. Called *Sole Survivor*, it was published by Lakeshore Charters and Marine Exploration in 1996. See also Hale's brief first-person account, "Survivor," *Inland Seas*, 51:2 (1995): 1–3. Hale spoke to reporters soon after his rescue and his story was carried by both the Associated Press and United Press International and published in most major newspapers on December 1 or 2, 1960 (depending on whether the newspaper was published in the morning or afternoon). On December 3, wire services carried a short article on the discovery of the wreck of the *Daniel J. Morrell*. The Coast Guard inquiry into the loss of the ship began December 5, 1960. Reports of the inquiry were carried by news services. Hale's lawsuit against the ship's owner, Bethlehem Steel Company, was reported by the Associated Press on December 9, 1960.